Upgrade
your Spanish

Upgrade
your Spanish

Abigail Lee Six

ROYAL HOLLOWAY
UNIVERSITY OF LONDON

A member of the
Hodder Headline Group
LONDON
Co-published in the United States of America
by Oxford University Press, Inc., New York

First published in Great Britain in 2001 by
Arnold, a member of the Hodder Headline Group,
338 Euston Road, London NW1 3BH

http://www.arnoldpublishers.com

Co-published in the United States of America by
Oxford University Press Inc.,
198 Madison Avenue, New York, NY10016

The advice and information in this book are believed to be true and
accurate at the date of going to press, but neither the author[s] nor the publisher
can accept any legal responsibility or liability for any errors or omissions.

British Library Cataloguing in Publication Data
A catalogue record for this book is available from the British Library

Library-of-Congress Cataloging-in-Publication Data
A catalog record for this book is available from the Library of Congress

ISBN 0 340 76186 5

1 2 3 4 5 6 7 8 9 10

Production Editor: Anke Ueberberg
Production Controller: Martin Kerans
Cover Design: Terry Griffiths
Illustrations: Colin Wheeler (chapter openers), Gejo Casanovas (illustrations)

Typeset in Formata by J&L Composition Ltd, Filey, North Yorkshire
Printed and bound in Malta by Gutenberg Press Ltd

What do you think about this book? Or any other Arnold title?
Please send your comments to feedback.arnold@hodder.co.uk

Contents

Acknowledgements   vi
Introduction   vii

Day 1:	Agreements	1
Day 2:	Describing People	7
Day 3:	Easy Subjunctive Constructions	13
Day 4:	Accents, Part I	17
Day 5:	Politics and Current Affairs	21
Day 6:	Regular Verbs	25
Day 7:	Visual Arts	31
Day 8:	Accents, Part II	37
Day 9:	Literature	43
Day 10:	*Ser* and *Estar*	51
Day 11:	Geography	57
Day 12:	Time	63
Day 13:	Rhetorical Signposts	69
Day 14:	History	75
Day 15:	Radical-changing Verbs	79
Day 16:	Music	85
Day 17:	Dependent Prepositions	91
Day 18:	Cinema	97
Day 19:	Irregular Verbs	101
Day 20:	Education	111
Day 21:	Conditional Sentences	117
Day 22:	Health	123
Day 23:	Dialogue	127
Day 24:	Spelling Changes	133
Day 25:	Science	137
Day 26:	Imperatives	143
Day 27:	Similes and Set Expressions	149
Day 28:	Minor Points	153
Day 29:	Vocabulary Test	159
Day 30:	Grammar Test	161

Progress Chart   164
Answers to Exercises   165
Index   177

Acknowledgements

I should like to thank my former and present institutions, Queen Mary & Westfield College and Royal Holloway, for granting me sabbatical leave to write *Upgrade*. I am grateful to my students for their willingness to be guinea-pigs when I was trying out different learning and revision strategies. Finally, I thank my two young sons, for the hours they let me spend at my desk instead of being with them.

Abigail Lee Six

Introduction

Upgrade is a thirty-day home revision and consolidation programme for Spanish language students at all levels from the sixth form to the final year of university or college. If you are not confident of getting an 'A' grade in your Spanish language examinations, this book can help you. Bearing in mind that you will have other subjects to revise in the vacation prior to your examinations, each day's exercises are designed to take between half an hour and one hour to complete. If you work through *Upgrade* seriously, you can improve your grade, so, for example, if you are likely to get a C without using the book, you can expect at least a B by studying it conscientiously.

AIMS OF THE BOOK

At this late stage, and working on your own, it is unrealistic to expect yourself for the first time to master the most complex and subtle aspects of the Spanish language; whatever progress you were going to make on those fronts has already been achieved. So, fascinating as these aspects are, *Upgrade* steers clear of them and focuses instead on the basics at the expense of the finer distinctions and the juicier exceptions to each rule.

This book does not aim to cover everything – a reference grammar and a dictionary serve that purpose – but instead to focus on three key areas where you can make a real difference in this last month:

– eliminating basic errors and slips of the pen;
– expanding and consolidating your vocabulary;
– injecting some sophistication into the style of your Spanish.

Keeping concentration at the optimum level is a major concern during uninterrupted hours of home revision. With this in mind and because you have dictionaries and reference grammars for systematic and ordered information, *Upgrade* may seem oddly random to you in its structure. Vocabulary is not in alphabetical order and grammar rules are covered only as and when they are thought to be of value to you, on your own, at the eleventh hour. The sections alternate between grammar and vocabulary, with style sections placed at longer intervals. All these varied and apparently random qualities are intended to keep you awake! But if you prefer to copy information into your own notes ordered differently, that in itself will be a good learning strategy. However, the daily exercises are designed to consolidate and build on work covered on previous days, so you should follow the order of the book to obtain the best results from it.

GETTING THE MOST FROM THIS BOOK

Different students will find different days harder than others, so don't be surprised if you can get a top score relatively effortlessly on one day, while another is a battle. This is simply because people's strengths and weaknesses differ. Remember that you are not wasting your time if you find certain exercises easy: you are consolidating, building confidence and learning where your particular strengths lie, all of which are very important aspects of preparation for examinations.

If you complete the exercises for one day in under half an hour, it is advisable not to go straight on to the next day's section. Do some language revision of your own (for example, past papers or your own vocabulary lists and notes) to make up the time you have allotted to language work, and come back to *Upgrade* tomorrow. On the other hand, if you find that you have not finished a particular day's exercises after about half an hour, it is best to stop anyway and come back to it later on, when you will have a new lease of concentration. Doggedly plodding on past saturation point is not the best way to achievement. So switch to another type of revision altogether and leave language work for at least an hour. You may like to work in pencil so that if you do find the exercises for a certain day particularly difficult, you can rub your answers out and try it all over again after an interval.

HOW THE EXERCISES WORK

The daily exercises carry 30 points each, numbered 1–30 with arabic numerals. All other sequences are numbered using roman numerals.

Where an exercise consists of filling gaps with Spanish words, the number of letters for each word you are looking for is shown by the number of blanks, thus: _ _ _ for a three-lettered word, for example. Where you are being asked to provide English words, a dotted line will be used, thus: .... , with no indication of word-lengths.

A sound will be presented within oblique strokes, thus: /g/. A letter of the alphabet, by contrast, will be in bold type, thus: **g**. Where the stressed vowel in a word needs to be shown, it will be underlined, thus: Isab<u>e</u>l.

Use the answer section to mark your own work and then put each day's score on the progress chart at the end of the book.

Never forget another agreement!

Do you ever forget to make your adjectives agree? Most students do. Here are some exercises to help you remember without fail, and some to give you practice at checking your work effectively by training your eye to spot forgotten agreements.

AGREEMENTS FOR GENDER
Not all adjectives have a different form for masculine and feminine. Here is a basic list of the ones that do:

▶ Those that end in -**o** in the masculine change to -**a** in the feminine, e.g. **bonito** [pretty] becomes **bonita**.

▶ Those that end in -**dor** in the masculine change to -**dora** in the feminine, e.g. **hablador** [talkative] becomes **habladora**.

▶ Those that end in -**án**, -**ín**, -**ón** or -**és** in the masculine, change to -**ana**, -**ina**, -**ona**, -**esa** in the feminine (NB: no accent in the feminine endings), e.g. **holgazán** [lazy] becomes **holgazana**, **pequeñín** [tiny] becomes **pequeñina**, **besucón** [liking to kiss] becomes **besucona**, and **francés** [French] becomes **francesa**.

Add the correct ending to the following:

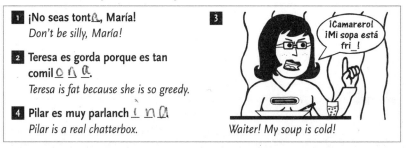

1 ¡No seas tont⌒, María!
Don't be silly, María!

2 Teresa es gorda porque es tan
comil○∩⌒.
Teresa is fat because she is so greedy.

4 Pilar es muy parlanch⌒∩⌒
Pilar is a real chatterbox.

3 ¡Camarero! ¡Mi sopa está fri_!

Waiter! My soup is cold!

AGREEMENTS FOR NUMBER
The basic rule is that adjectives ending in a vowel add **s**; adjectives ending in a consonant add -**es**. If there is a written accent on the last syllable of the adjective, remember that it will often lose it when you pluralize because you will have added a syllable to the end of the word (e.g. **inglés** becomes **ingleses**). Don't touch an accent anywhere else, though. Stress rules will be covered more thoroughly on Day 8. Adjectives ending in **z** will change it to **c** before adding **es** (e.g. **voraz** [voracious] becomes **voraces**), but you will have a chance to think about spelling changes like this again on Day 24.

A few adjectives do not have a plural form; often this is because they are really nouns. An example is **naranja** [orange]. This is too complicated to go into here. However, a good idea in these cases is to turn the phrase around, so, for example, to translate 'orange flowers', say **flores de color naranja.**

To get agreements right every time,

▶ first make any agreement necessary for gender;

▶ then pluralize if required.

Thus, to describe **mujeres** [women] with the adjectives **inteligente** [clever] and **bonito** [pretty]:

Step 1   Make each adjective feminine if it has a feminine form: **inteligente + bonita** – (**inteligente** does not end in -**o**, so there is no change for the feminine form).

Step 2   Make each adjective plural. Both end in a vowel so both just add **s**: **mujeres inteligentes y bonitas.**

Complete the following adjectives:

5 Mis hijas son muy trabaja**doras**. *My daughters are very hard-working.*	**6** Tengo que darte noticias important**es**. *I have to give you some important news.*	**7** Estos ejercicios son fácil**es**. *These exercises are easy.*

Now practise your checking strategy

Read the following passage, imagining you wrote it yourself in an examination and are now checking it through. Find each adjective and check whether or not it agrees with its noun as it should. Correct it if necessary. Tick the ones you think are correct as they stand, to prove to yourself that you <u>have</u> considered them.

---

8 – **13**   Al volver a la Universidad después de una estancia de tres años en Puerto Rico, Pedro Salinas escribió alguno ensayos de crítica literaria y puso el toque final a algunos piezas teatrales, pero sobre todo, en los últimos años de su vida, se concentró en la prosa narrativo. Publicó su relato orwelliano, *La bomba impecable*, y luchó con aquella novela que tanto trabajo le costaba, titulado provisionalmente 'El valor de la vida', novela sobre el tema de la guerra que, por fin, dejó inacabado.

How many corrections have you made? If you found six, score 6 points and go on to the next exercise. If you found fewer (or more!) than six, try again before consulting the answer section; then take off a mark for every one you missed or 'corrected' when it was really right.

COMMON CONFUSIONS OVER AGREEMENTS

I Past participles

These (e.g. **hablado**, **dicho** or, as above, **titulado**) do not agree when they are part of a compound tense (i.e. one made up of two words), conjugated with **haber**. The rest of the time they do agree. For example:

Rocío había hablado con el profesor sobre el asunto.
[Rocío had spoken to the teacher about the matter.]

▶ No agreement because **había hablado** is the pluperfect, a compound tense conjugated with **haber**.

Esta novela fue escrita en 1907. [This novel was written in 1907.]

▶ Agrees because the past participle (**escrito**) is with **ser** (**fue**), not **haber**.

La puerta está cerrada. [The door is shut.]

▶ Agrees because the past participle (**cerrado**) is with **estar** (**está**), not **haber**.

Complete the unfinished words below, making agreements where necessary:

---

14 – 16 **La ensalada había sid_o_ preparad_a_ con muchos ingredientes exótic_o s_.**
Lots of exotic ingredients had been used to make the salad.

17 **Las chicas tienen que haber terminad_o_ estos ejercicios antes de las 10.**
The girls need to have finished these exercises by ten o'clock.

18, **19** **Tengo leíd_a s_ cien páginas, pero Cecilia ha leíd_o_ la novela entera ya.**
I've got through a hundred pages, but Cecilia has already read the whole novel.

II Present participles

These (e.g. **hablando** [speaking], **comiendo** [eating]) do not agree: **María y Juana están hablando** – never **hablandas** [Maria and Juana are speaking].
Note that they should never be confused with past participles:

La puerta está abierta. [The door is open.]

▶ Must agree because the past participle (**abierta**) is conjugated with **estar**.

La puerta se ha abierto. [The door has opened.]

▶ Does not agree because the past participle (**abierto**) is conjugated with **haber** (**ha**).

La puerta se está abriendo. [The door is opening.]

▶ Does not agree because **abriendo** is a present participle.

Tick the correct sentences and correct any that have errors of agreement in them:

20	La tienda estaba cerrada. ✓
	cerrando
21, **22**	La tienda se estaba cerranda cuando llegó corriendo mi madre.
23	La casa fue destrozada por el incendio.
24, **25**	La abuela tiene guardado mucho recuerdos de su juventud.
26, **27**	Las nietas no habían visto nunca tantas cosas bonitas.

Have you made five corrections? If not, reread the guidelines before the exercise and then give yourself one more chance before turning to the answer section to add up your score.

III **Demasiado** [too much] agrees when it is used as an adjective but does not agree when it is used as an adverb.
Remember that adverbs tell you more about verbs, adjectives and other adverbs.

For example:

Ana habla demasiado. [Ana talks too much.]
▶ No agreement because **demasiado** is telling you more about the verb **hablar**, so it is an adverb here.

Conchita es demasiado tonta para comprenderlo.
[Conchita is too stupid to understand.]
▶ No agreement because **demasiado** is telling you more about the adjective **tonta**, so that means it is an adverb here too.

No se puede tener demasiados amigos. [You can't have too many friends.]
▶ Agrees because in this sentence **demasiado** is telling you more about a noun, **amigos**, which means it is an adjective.

Now try these:

28 Estoy demasiado cansada para hacerlo. *I am too tired to do it.*	**29** Lourdes ha puesto demasiada sal en el arroz. *Lourdes has put too much salt in the rice.*	**30** No bebas demasiado, Amparo. *Don't drink too much, Amparo.*

Was any of the vocabulary in this section unfamiliar to you? If so, have you noted it? Make sure you have listed any nouns with their gender and any verbs with their irregularities and dependent prepositions (if any).

If you know you have a tendency to miss agreements, especially in a stressful situation like an examination, make sure you leave time to check through any Spanish you have written, looking purely at the agreements.

Now check whether your answers are correct. If you scored 30 out of 30, you can consider this section finished. If you scored less than 20 out of 30, you should do it all over again, but not now. Do something else for at least an hour before coming back to it. If you scored between 20 and 29 out of 30, look back tomorrow at the mistakes you have made before starting the next section. Be sure you understand where and why you went wrong before moving on. Follow this procedure for each day you work on *Upgrade*.

Don't expect a book of this kind to provide you with all the vocabulary you might need in an examination. The aim of Upgrade *is a different one: it is intended to consolidate some words and phrases you know already and to link them to others that have the same origin. These etymologically associated items are called 'cognates'.*

Making links between such words should help you in three main ways:

a) to expand your vocabulary;

b) to provide you with a technique for accelerating your acquisition of vocabulary in the future, after the immediate threat of examinations has passed. If you make a point of always learning a new word alongside one or two others that are cognate, you will get two or three items for hardly more than the 'price' of one;

c) to build up your understanding of how the Spanish language is constructed, enabling you to guess more confidently at words you have not come across before. For example, if you had learnt **la democracia** [democracy] alongside **democrático** [democratic] and **el/la demócrata** [democrat)], then you would find it quite easy if the need arose, to guess that **aristócrata** must be 'aristocrat', rather than, say, 'aristocratic' and even perhaps to risk inventing how to say 'aristocrat' actively when writing or speaking Spanish.

This type of knowledge will not only help you in examinations, but also enable you to read faster and more accurately, comprehend the spoken language better and, above all, contribute to developing that all-important but elusive 'feel' for Spanish.

Here are ten groups of words relating to the physical description of people. You will probably know at least one in each group already. Try to learn any of the others that you do not know by linking them in your mind to the one(s) you do. Then practise using some of them by sketching appropriate features on the blank faces next to the sentences at the end of the list on page 8. To consolidate the agreement rules in yesterday's section, the endings have been left off the adjectives in the sentences, for you to complete.

el rizo curl
rizado curly
rizar to curl
liso straight (of hair), smooth (of skin or surface)
alisar to smooth

✓**las cejas** eyebrows
fruncir las cejas to frown
✓**arquear las cejas** to raise one's eyebrows
✓ **cejijunto** with eyebrows that meet in the middle

el pelo hair
peludo hairy
peliagudo tricky (in sense of difficult)
no tener pelos en la lengua not to mince one's words
con el pelo al rape with cropped hair

la barba beard, chin
dejar la barba to grow a beard
barbudo bearded
la barbilla (tip of the) chin

la nariz nose
narigudo with a big nose
estar hasta las narices de . . . to be fed up to the back teeth with . . .
en sus propias narices right in his/her/their face

la boca mouth
desembocar to flow (river) into, come out (street) into
boquiabierto open-mouthed (with astonishment)
una bocanada puff (e.g. of smoke)
boquear to gasp (used for fish when taken out of water), therefore used figuratively for 'to be at death's door'.

la cara face
tener cara de sueño to look tired
encararse con to face up to, confront
descarado cheeky, shameless
¡Qué cara! What a cheek!

el ojo eye
¡ojo! watch out!
las ojeras bags or rings under one's eyes
el ojal buttonhole
costar un ojo de la cara to cost an arm and a leg

la frente forehead (NB not to be confused with **el frente** military or weather front)
tener la frente despejada to have a high forehead

Boquiabierta ... en sus propias narices

Now practise as outlined above.

1 – 2   Este chico tiene la frente despejad_ y el pelo al rape.

4 – 5   Este barbudo está frunciendo las cejas.

3   Esta chica tiene el pelo lis_ y larg_.

6 – 7   ¡Qué cara de sueño tiene este hombre!
¡Mira las ojeras que tiene!

8 Esta mujer está boquiabierta; acaba de llegarle una noticia muy sorprendente.

9–**10** Este narigudo está arqueando las cejas.

11 Ninguno de estos niños tiene el pelo rizado.

Check your answers against the answer section. Score an extra point **12** if you got all the agreements right.

Now, here are ten groups of words relating to character. Again, you will probably know at least one in each group already. Use that knowledge to make learning the rest easier.

el **humor** mood
malhumorado bad-tempered

suave gentle
suavizar to soften, calm
el **suavizante** hair conditioner, fabric softener

la **pereza** laziness, lethargy
perezoso lazy
desperezarse to stretch (as on first waking up)

el **orgullo** pride
orgulloso proud

el **pudor** modesty (especially sexual)
púdico modest
pudibundo prudish

terco stubborn
la **terquedad** stubbornness

la **índole** disposition, nature
de **buena/mala índole** good/bad-natured

frívolo frivolous
la **frivolidad** frivolity

tacaño miserly, mean (with money), stingy
la **tacañería** miserliness, meanness, stinginess

la **vergüenza** shame, embarrassment
un **sinvergüenza** shameless person, good-for-nothing
desvergonzado shameless

Now practise by doing this wordfit puzzle. Each time you fit a word into the grid, copy it against its meaning opposite. (Here's a clue – start with the longest word first!) The shaded squares will give you the letters for one word that is missing from the grid. Note that all nouns should appear with their definite article in the grid. You should only count the answer as correct if you have got the article right too and remembered any accents.

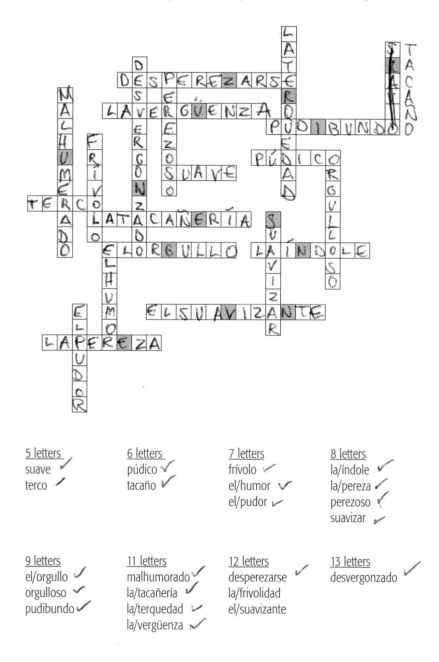

5 letters
suave
terco

6 letters
púdico
tacaño

7 letters
frívolo
el/humor
el/pudor

8 letters
la/índole
la/pereza
perezoso
suavizar

9 letters
el/orgullo
orgulloso
pudibundo

11 letters
malhumorado
la/tacañería
la/terquedad
la/vergüenza

12 letters
desperezarse
la/frivolidad
el/suavizante

13 letters
desvergonzado

13	mood	el humor
	bad-tempered	malhumorado
14	gentle	suave
	to soften	suavizar
	hair conditioner	el suavizante
15	laziness, lethargy	la pereza
	lazy	perezoso
	to stretch	desperezarse
16	shame	la vergüenza
	good-for-nothing	un sinvergüenza
	shameless	desvergonzado
17	pride	el orgullo
	proud	orgulloso
18	modesty	el pudor
	modest	púdico
	prudish	pudibundo
19	stubborn	terco
	stubbornness	la terquedad
20	disposition	la índole
21	frivolous	frívolo
	frivolity	la frivolidad
22	miserly	tacaño
	miserliness	la tacañería

The following vocabulary group is linked to clothing. Once you think you have learnt it all, test yourself by trying to complete the sentences.

la camisa shirt	**los tejanos/vaqueros** jeans
la camiseta tee-shirt or vest	**tejano** Texan or denim
el camisón nightdress	**la vaca** cow
en mangas de camisa in shirtsleeves	**el vaquero** cowboy
descamisado ragged, or follower of General Perón of Argentina	BUT **la americana** sports jacket
	los zapatos shoes
el abrigo overcoat or shelter	**las zapatillas** slippers/ballet shoes/sports shoes
abrigar to shelter ('give shelter to')	**zapatear** to stamp or tap one's feet
abrigarse to wrap up warm	BUT **el zapatista** follower of Zapata in Mexican Revolution
los calcetines socks	
hacer calceta to knit (old-fashioned expression; **hacer punto** used more nowadays)	**el gorro** hat (informal type without brim, e.g. woolly)
descalzo barefoot	**la gorra de visera** peaked cap
calzarse to put on (of footwear)	**pasar la gorra** to pass the hat around (i.e. to beg)
el cinturón belt	**gorrear** to scrounge
la cintura waist	
abrocharse el cinturón de seguridad to fasten one's seat-belt	**el traje** outfit, suit
	el traje de luces bullfighter's outfit

Now complete the sentences and then check your answers in the answers section:

23 Se ruega a los señores pasajeros que *se abrochan los cinturones de seguridad*
Passengers are requested to fasten their seatbelts.

24 Se compró dos *camisones* nuev⊕s en las rebajas.
She bought herself two new nightdresses in the sales.

25–26 Llevaba *tejanos/vaqueros* y una *gorra de visera*. *He was wearing jeans and a peaked cap.*

27 *Abrígate*, que hace frío. *It's cold, so wrap up well (tú form).*

28 El *traje* de novia de Adelaida era magnífic⊕.
Adelaida's wedding-dress was magnificent.

29 No me gusta que los niños anden *descalzos*, por si se resfrían. *I don't like the children to be barefoot in case they catch cold.*

30 El público *zapatea* en señal de protesta.
The audience stamped their feet in protest.

Upgrade your style: Easy but elegant constructions using the subjunctive

Most students shudder at any mention of the subjunctive and it is true that some aspects of its use in Spanish are difficult to master. However, there are plenty of subjunctive constructions that are easy to use and if you acquire the habit of doing so, your written style in Spanish will be significantly improved. The constructions in this section all demand the subjunctive (i.e. the indicative is impossible); this means that you do not have to decide between indicative and subjunctive, which is usually the trickiest part.

Here are some examples.

I **Ojalá** + present subjunctive is an expression of hope
e.g. **Ojalá venga pronto.** [I hope/let's hope he/she comes soon.]

II **Ojalá** + pluperfect subjunctive expresses 'if only . . .'
e.g. **Ojalá me lo hubieras dicho antes.** [If only you had told me before.]

III **Como si** + past subjunctives expresses 'as if '/ 'as though'
e.g. **Me habla/habló como si fuera mi padre**. [He speaks/spoke to me as if he were my father.]
Note that in colloquial English we could easily say 'He speaks to me as if he is my father', but that is in fact incorrect and is not used in Spanish.

IV **Por** + adjective + **que** + subjunctive is a special construction
e.g. **Por ridículo que pueda parecer** . . . [Ridiculous as it may seem . . .]; **Por mucho que me lo ruegues, no lo haré.** [No matter how much you beg me, I shan't do it.]

V **Forma reduplicativa**
e.g. **Sea como sea** . . . [Be that as it may . . .]; **Vaya donde vaya** . . . [Wherever he/she goes . . .]

VI **Dicho sea de paso** – literally, 'let it be said in passing', a set expression to introduce an incidental point
e.g. **Esta cuestión tiene mucho peso político y, dicho sea de paso, no solamente en España.** [This matter carries much political weight and, incidentally / one might add, not just in Spain.]

VII **Quizá** followed by subjunctive expresses 'perhaps' at the more unlikely end of the spectrum of possibility
Note that the subjunctive is necessary only when **quizá** comes before the verb. To make your written Spanish more elegant, why not make a point of putting it there?
e.g. **Quizá venga mañana.** [*Perhaps he/she will come tomorrow.*]

Now practise using these constructions in the sentences below.

---

1 **Hagas lo que hagas**, te querré siempre.
Whatever you do, I'll always love you. (Use **tú**.)

2 **Ojalá** me **hubiera hecho caso**,
entonces nada de esto habría sucedido.
If only he had listened to me, none of this would have happened.
(Hint: use **hacer caso** for 'listened' in this context.)

3 **Quizá** la vuelv**a** a ver un día.
Perhaps I'll see her again one day.

4 Por poco probable **que pueda parecer**, le
reconocí la voz en seguida.
Improbable as it may seem, I recognized her voice at once.

5 Tenía el pelo tan desmelenad**o**, era como si llev**ara** semanas sin
peinarse.
Her hair was so messy, it was as if she had not combed it in weeks.

6 **Ojalá** no se **descubra** nunca la verdad.
Let's hope the truth is never discovered.

7 Es un gran novelista y, **dicho sea de paso**, su
esposa no le va a la zaga.
He is a great novelist and, by the way, so is his wife.

Are you in danger of misreading an indicative as a subjunctive or vice-versa? If you make this mistake you could misunderstand a whole sentence (or plot of a novel!). Consider, for example, these two sentences that might be crucial in a detective story:

No lo maté porque era mi hermano.
No lo maté porque fuera mi hermano.

In the first sentence the speaker did not kill his/her brother and the reason was because it was his/her brother. In the second sentence, the speaker <u>did</u> kill his/her brother but the reason was unrelated to the fact that it was his/her brother.

Might you aim for a subjunctive but accidentally write the indicative or vice versa? You will have a chance to practise your verb forms on Days 6, 15, and 19, but for now try this quick check to find out how much attention you need to give to the subject. Ring S for subjunctive or I for the indicative, after each of the following verb forms. You should not have to stare and stare at them to work it out; if you do, you do not know your verbs well enough.

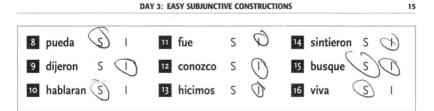

8	pueda	S	I	**11**	fue	S		
9	dijeron	S	I	**12**	conozco	S	I	
10	hablaran	S	I	**13**	hicimos	S	I	

14	sintieron	S	I
15	busque	S	I
16	viva	S	I

Are you apt to forget to use the subjunctive in any of the constructions practised in this section? The following sentences contain some errors of this kind. Try to spot and then correct them as you would if you were checking through your own written Spanish. There may be some missed agreements too, so check through, twice at least, before looking up the answer section.

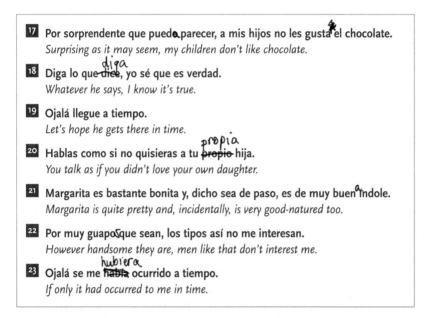

A mis hijos no les gusta el chocolate

---

17 Por sorprendente que pueda parecer, a mis hijos no les gusta el chocolate.
Surprising as it may seem, my children don't like chocolate.

18 Diga lo que diga, yo sé que es verdad.
Whatever he says, I know it's true.

19 Ojalá llegue a tiempo.
Let's hope he gets there in time.

20 Hablas como si no quisieras a tu propia hija.
You talk as if you didn't love your own daughter.

21 Margarita es bastante bonita y, dicho sea de paso, es de muy buena índole.
Margarita is quite pretty and, incidentally, is very good-natured too.

22 Por muy guapos que sean, los tipos así no me interesan.
However handsome they are, men like that don't interest me.

23 Ojalá se me hubiera ocurrido a tiempo.
If only it had occurred to me in time.

Finally, for today, put the infinitive in parentheses into its correct form for the following sentences and check your answers in the answers section.

---

24 Esa chica trata mi casa como si (ser) fuera la suya.
That girl treats my house as if it were her own.

25 (Ir) Vayas donde vayas, yo te seguiré.
Wherever you go, I'll follow.

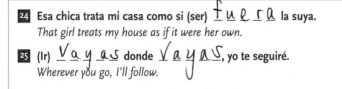

26 Ojalá (encontrar [nosotros]) _encontremos_ la oportunidad
para pasar más tiempo juntos en los años que vienen.
Let us hope we have the chance to spend more time together in years to come.

27 Por absurdo que te (poder) _pueda_ parecer a primera vista, mi
decisión es final.
Absurd as it may seem to you at first glance, my decision is final.

28 Tu argumento me parece frívolo y, _dicho sea de paso_,
esta actitud arrogante que tienes tampoco me impresiona.
*I find your argument frivolous and, by the way, that arrogant attitude of yours
doesn't impress me either.*

29 Quizá (ser) _sea_ mejor así.
Maybe it's better like this.

30 Ojalá me lo (explicar) _hubieras explicado_
antes de ir corriendo a tu madre.
If only you had explained it to me before you went running to your mother.

Stop losing marks for accents!
Part I: Accents for reasons other than stress rules

Accents are notorious mark-losers for students in examinations. But resist the temptation to be defeatist about this: you can avoid all errors concerning accents if you make your mind up to it this month. For some students this alone can improve their mark by a whole grade!

ACCENTS IN THE INTERROGATIVE/EXCLAMATORY FORMS
There are three possible reasons for putting a written accent on a word in Spanish.

I **To indicate an interrogative or exclamatory form**
e.g. **¿Qué haces?** [What are you doing?]; **¡Qué risa!** [How funny!]

II **To distinguish between certain pairs of monosyllabic words** that have different meanings but would otherwise look identical
e.g. **No me gusta el té.** [I don't like <u>tea</u>.]; **Te quiero.** [I love <u>you</u>.]

III **To indicate where the stress falls** on a word which does not obey the stress rules of Spanish e.g. **difícil** [difficult]

The exercises for today cover the first type. The third will be the subject of Day 8's exercises.

The basic rules for the first use
i) Interrogatives carry an accent (placed on the stressed vowel), even in indirect questions. For example:

¿Cómo te llamas? [What is your name?]
▶ Direct question using the interrogative adverb **¿<u>cómo</u>?**

¿Cuánto dinero tienes? [How much money have you got?]
▶ Direct question using the interrogative adjective **¿<u>cuánto</u>?** (here **cuánto** is an adjective because it is telling you more about **dinero**).

No sé cómo se llama.
[I don't know what his name is.]
▶ Indirect question using the interrogative adverb.

Me pregunto cuánto dinero tiene.
[I wonder how much money she's got.]
▶ Indirect question using an interrogative adjective.

ii) Exclamatory adjectives and pronouns carry an accent on the stressed vowel. For example:

¡Qué vestido más bonito! [What a pretty dress!]
¡Cuánto me gusta! [I love it!] (Lit. 'How much it pleases me!')

Note that Spanish uses exclamatory forms more than English. A literal translation is very often inappropriate, as in this example.

Choose a suitable word to fill each of the gaps in the following interrogative and exclamatory sentences. To keep practising agreements, the endings of adjectives will also need to be added.

1	¿**Dónde** compraste es_a_ camiseta tan origin_ _? *Where did you buy that unusual tee-shirt?*
2	¿**Que** le dijiste para suavizar un poco la mal_a_ noticia? *What did you say to soften the bad news a little?*
3 – 4	No recuerdo _dónde_ ni _cuándo_ la conocí. *I don't recall where or when I met her.*
5	¡**Qué** horror! *How awful!*
6	¡**Cuánta** gente mal educad_o_ por aquí! *The people round here are so rude!*

The most common pitfall
This is to confuse a relative with an interrogative. (If it is any consolation, native speakers get this wrong too!)
Remember that not all questions contain an interrogative pronoun, adjective or adverb. This type of question is usually called a 'closed question', because it can be answered simply by 'yes' or 'no'. The type of question introduced by an interrogative is usually known as an 'open question'. For example:

¿Conoces a mi novio, Juan? [Do you know my boyfriend, Juan?]
▶ Closed question because yes/no answer is possible.

¿Quién eres? [Who are you?]

▶ Open question because yes/no answer is not possible.

A closed question of the yes/no type might happen to contain a relative pronoun:

¿Has visto el coche que compré ayer?
[Have you seen the car (that) I bought yesterday?]

If you find this confusing, think about the English translation of the closed sentence above: the relative pronoun **que** is translated by 'that' but it can be left out altogether in English. The interrogative form, however, would have been translated by 'what' and could not have been left out. This tip is given to help you get a feel for the difference between relative and interrogative pronouns. But *note* it is not a foolproof mechanism for identifying them.

A closed question might also happen to contain an indirect question. Consider the following:

¿Dónde viven tus padres? [Where do your parents live?]

▶ Direct open question.

¿Conoces el barrio donde viven mis padres?
[Do you know the neighbourhood my parents live in?]

▶ Direct closed question, happening to contain a relative adverb (**donde**). It can be omitted altogether in the English translation, which helps to identify it as a relative and not an interrogative.

¿Sabes dónde viven? [Do you know where they live?]

▶ Direct closed question, happening to contain an indirect question, hence the accent on **dónde**. Note that here the **dónde** has to be translated; this helps to identify it as an interrogative and not a relative.

Practise making these distinctions between relatives and interrogatives in direct and indirect questions by putting accents on the words that require them below. *Remember* to keep practising the agreements on adjectives.

7-**8**   **¿Por qué me tratas así? ¿Es porque no me quieres ya?**
  Why are you treating me like this? Is it because you don't love me any more?

9-**12**   **¿Cuántos veces tendré que repetirte que eso no tiene nada que ver?**
  How many times will I have to repeat that that's got nothing to do with it?

13   **No sé cómo te atreves a emplear este tono agresivo conmigo.**
  I don't know how you dare use that aggressive tone to me.

14-**15**   **¿Así que el fontanero no llegó hasta las seis? ¡Qué pesadilla!**
  So the plumber didn't get there until six o'clock? What a nightmare!

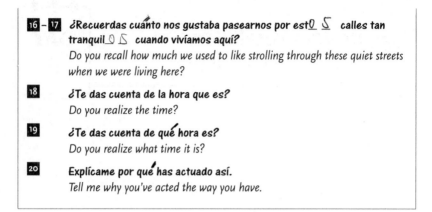

16 – **17** ¿Recuerdas cuánto nos gustaba pasearnos por est_0_ _S_ calles tan
tranquil_0_ _S_ cuando vivíamos aquí?
*Do you recall how much we used to like strolling through these quiet streets
when we were living here?*

18   ¿Te das cuenta de la hora que es?
Do you realize the time?

19   ¿Te das cuenta de qué hora es?
Do you realize what time it is?

20   Explícame por qué has actuado así.
Tell me why you've acted the way you have.

Reminder: Are you still noting down any unfamiliar vocabulary that happens to appear in
these exercises? When you do, are you remembering to include the gender of nouns
and any irregularities or dependent prepositions of verbs?

Finally, match the following half sentences with their mate by connecting them with a
line and correct the accents where necessary. Some are correct, some are superfluous,
others are missing.

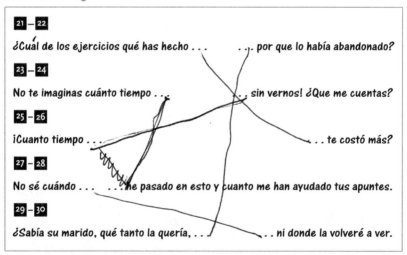

21 – **22**

¿Cuál de los ejercicios qué has hecho . . .   . . . por que lo había abandonado?

23 – **24**

No te imaginas cuánto tiempo . . .   . . . sin vernos! ¿Que me cuentas?

25 – **26**

¡Cuanto tiempo . . .   . . . te costó más?

27 – **28**

No sé cuándo . . .   . . . he pasado en esto y cuanto me han ayudado tus apuntes.

29 – **30**

¿Sabía su marido, qué tanto la quería, ... ni donde la volveré a ver.

To be comfortable when you talk, read, or write about politics and current affairs, you need to have sufficient vocabulary relating to both the Anglophone and Hispanic spheres. Obviously, this is an enormous lexical domain, far too extensive to cover fully in one day. But you can make sure you know some basic general terms. So the exercises for today will highlight a selection of these, along with some that focus on Spain, Britain, and Europe; if your particular needs are more transatlantic you could devise a parallel list to learn alongside, or instead of, some of those given here.

As before, vocabulary is given in related sets of terms so that you can learn by linking. Here are the first 10:

el gobierno government
el/la gobernador/-ora governor
gobernar (radical-changing – see Day 15) to govern
gubernamental governmental (note the 'u' in Spanish), e.g. **los organismos no gubernamentales** non-governmental organizations, NGOs
gobernante ruling, e.g. **la clase gobernante** the ruling class

las Cortes the Spanish Parliament
la corte (royal) court
hacerle la corte a alguien to woo / court s.o. (also fig.)

votar a to vote for
emitir su voto to cast one's vote
el voto vote, or religious vow
un voto a favor de algo a vote in favour of s.th.
un voto en contra de algo a vote against s.th. (Note the prepositions for this pair.)
el exvoto votive offering

las elecciones generales/municipales general/local election (Notice the plural in Spanish.)
elegir (radical-changing, as **pedir** – see Day 15) to elect, choose
la elección choice
el/la elector/-ora voter
el electorado the electorate
electoral election (adj.), as in **la campaña electoral** election campaign

el presupuesto the budget
el supuesto supposition, assumption
presuponer (irreg., as **poner** – see Day 19) to presuppose

la Cámara de los Comunes the House of Commons
la Cámara de los Lores the House of Lords
la cámara chamber
el/la cámara cameraman / camerawoman
el camarero/la camarera waiter/waitress; bellboy/hotel maid

la mayoría majority
mayoritario majority (adj.), as in **una decisión mayoritaria** – a majority decision
la minoría the minority
minoritario minority (adj.), as in **un gobierno minoritario** a minority government
llegar a la mayoría de edad to come of age

el mitin (political) meeting
el líder (political) leader
el liderazgo (political) leadership

el tratado treaty
el trato deal, as in **hacer un trato** to make a deal
estar en tratos con to be in negotiations with
de trato fácil easy-going

el (primer) ministro/la (primera) ministra the (Prime) Minister
el ministerio ministry
el consejo de ministros Council of Ministers (Sp. and EU); Cabinet (GB)

Once you think you have learnt these, practise by filling the gaps in the sentences below. To consolidate the work you did yesterday on rules for accents placed for reasons other than stress, some accents have been left off – so make sure you add them where necessary.

1 – 3 ¿A qué hora anoche llegó **el consejo de ministros** a un acuerdo sobre **el presupuesto** de la Unión Europea?
At what time last night did the Council of Ministers reach agreement on the budget of the EU?

4 – 6 En las reuniones de las Naciones Unidas, sé que **los organismos no gubernamentales** tienen el derecho de asistir pero ¿pueden **votar**?
I know that NGOs have the right to attend UN meetings but can they vote?

7 – 9 Al **primer ministro** de un **gobierno minoritario** le cuesta imponer el programa legislativo que ha prometido al **electorado**.
It is hard for the prime minister of a minority government to push through the legislative programme that he has promised the electorate.

10 La reforma de **la cámara de los lores** ha comenzado ya pero muchas cuestiones quedan por resolver.
Reform of the House of Lords has now begun but many questions have yet to be resolved.

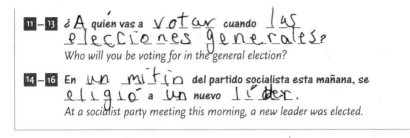

11–13 ¿A quién vas a *votar* cuando *las elecciones generales?*

Who will you be voting for in the general election?

14–16 En *un mitin* del partido socialista esta mañana, se *eligió* a *un* nuevo *líder.*

At a socialist party meeting this morning, a new leader was elected.

Here is a second set of terms. These have morphological rather than lexical links. In other words it is the form rather than the meaning which links the groups:

la democracia democracy
el/la demócrata democrat
democrático democratic
poco democrático undemocratic
la aristocracia aristocracy
el/la aristócrata aristocrat
aristocrático aristocratic

el senado senate or senate building/house
el/la senador/-ora senator
senatorial senatorial (note the 't' in Spanish)
el ecuador equator
ecuatorial equatorial
el estado state
estatal state (adj.), as in **una subvención estatal** state subsidy

el Partido Laborista Labour Party (GB)
el laborismo Labour movement
el/la laborista Labour supporter or party member
el Partido Comunista Communist Party
el comunismo communism
el/la comunista communist
el Partido Socialista Socialist Party
el socialismo socialism
el/la socialista socialist
BUT **el Partido Conservador** Conservative Party (GB)
el conservadurismo Conservatism
el/la conservador/-ora Conservative supporter or party member

de izquierdas left-wing
de derechas right-wing
de buenas a primeras all of a sudden

El mitin

Once you have learnt these, try to deduce how to say the following:

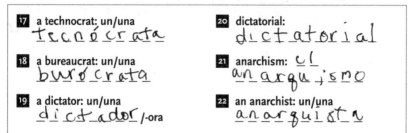

17 a technocrat: un/una
tecnócrata

18 a bureaucrat: un/una
burócrata

19 a dictator: un/una
dictador /-ora

20 dictatorial:
dictatorial

21 anarchism: *el*
anarquismo

22 an anarchist: un/una
anarquista

Find the best way to translate the following:

23 – 25 En el fondo es un político de derechas no obstante su imagen centro izquierdista.

Deep down, he is a right-wing politician not w/standing his center left image.

26 – 27 El conservadurismo británico no se parece mucho a la derecha política de los Estados Unidos.

British conservatism is quite unlike the pol. right in the U.S.

28 Las escuelas del sector estatal suelen tener clases más numerosas que las del sector privado.

Schools in the state sector tend to have larger classes than the private sector.

29 – 30 En el África ecuatorial, el tribalismo puede tener más importancia que las ideologías políticas.

In the African equatorial, tribalism can have more importance the political ideologies

Perfect precision with regular verb forms

Are you one of the many students who might make a mistake with a regular verb form? If so, it is not too late to remedy the problem and it is definitely worth making the effort to do so. All it takes is some clear thinking and the determination never to lose another mark for something as elementary as this.

The key to success is twofold:
▶ first, you have to know the three conjugations one hundred percent;
▶ second, you have to be able to match the verb you are trying to use to the right pattern.

Today, therefore, the first exercises are designed to help you ensure that you are rock solid on the forms of regular **-ar** (e.g. **hablar** [to speak]), **-er** (e.g. **comer** [to eat]), and **-ir** (e.g. **vivir** [to live]) verbs. Then there will be a chance to practise the best technique for always going to the right conjugation for each verb you are using.

Remember that if you find reciting verbs helpful as a way to memorize them, you *must* pronounce them correctly to yourself – whether in your head or aloud. The temptation is to place the stress on the ending. But if you do that with a verb whose correct pronunciation stresses the stem, you will have spelling problems with accents. You will improve your spoken Spanish, and help yourself enormously with spelling, if you make sure that you use your best accent at all times, even when you are just mumbling verbs to yourself. As well as looking at where the stress falls in each form, this also means differentiating between a single and double 'r' sound – for example, reciting **narrar** [to narrate] or **parar** [to stop].

In this section, the stressed vowel will be underlined so that you can check on your pronunciation as well as your spelling.

I   Present indicative

hablar	comer	vivir
hablo	como	vivo
hablas	comes	vives
habla	come	vive
hablamos	comemos	vivimos
habláis	coméis	vivís
hablan	comen	viven

Notice that there is a certain logic to these forms: it might help you to bear in mind that the most straightforward tense and mood – the present indicative – features **a** in the endings of **-ar** verbs and **e** in the endings of **-er** verbs, and **i** figures strongly in the endings of **-ir** verbs.

II   Present subjunctive

Remember that the present subjunctive (you can think of it as being perverse if it helps!), makes **-ar** verbs look a bit like **-er** ones and makes **-er** and **-ir** verbs look rather like **-ar** ones.

hablar	comer	vivir
hable	coma	viva
hables	comas	vivas
hable	coma	viva
hablemos	comamos	vivamos
habléis	comáis	viváis
hablen	coman	vivan

Of course you know all this, so why do you still sometimes get it wrong? Is it because you are not systematic enough when writing down a verb form? Follow these steps and you can eliminate the mistakes.

To get the present subjunctive right every time, ask yourself:

Step 1   What is the infinitive of the verb I want to use?

Step 2   What tense and mood am I aiming for?

Step 3   Is it regular? If so, I match it to the appropriate form of **hablar**, **comer**, or **vivir**. Is it radical-changing? If so, I match it to the appropriate form of **entender** [to understand], **mentir** [to lie], or **pedir** [to ask for].

Step 4   Is it irregular? If so, I must call on my memory to know how to conjugate it.

The following common mistakes arise from a lack of thinking clearly through the four steps outlined above:

▶ confusing **crear**, the regular **-ar** verb meaning 'to create', with **creer**, the irregular **-er** verb meaning 'to believe'; and

▶ confusing **sentarse** the regular (but radical-changing) **-ar** verb meaning 'to sit down', with **sentirse** the regular (but radical-changing) **-ir** verb meaning 'to feel'.

Practise the regular present indicative and subjunctive forms by first trying to write out the three conjugations from memory until you have been able to do so faultlessly, at least twice in succession.

Now try these:

1 ¿Quieres que te cant_ mi última canción?

Would you like me to sing you my latest song?

2 ¿Dónde viv_ _ los González?
Where do the González family live?

3 No me levant_ nunca antes de las nueve.
I never get up before nine o'clock.

4 ¿Por qué dices que no me cre_? ¡Es la pura verdad!
Why are you saying you don't believe me? It's absolutely true!

5 Pas_ lo que pas_, puedes contar conmigo.
Whatever happens, you can count on me.

III Preterite

There is no need to reprint all the regular verb forms here; you can find them in a dictionary or a specialized verb reference book. Look through them now and write out any you feel you need to, as many times as necessary. Then try to fill in the table below from memory, underlining the stressed vowel:

	hablar	comer	vivir
6 (yo)	hablé	comí	viví
7 (tú)	hablaste	comiste	viviste
8 (él/ella)	habló	comió	vivió
9 (nosotros/-as)	hablamos	comimos	vivimos
10 (vosotros/-as)	_____	_____	_____
11 (ellos/ellas)	hablaron	comieron	vivieron

IV Imperfect subjunctive

Now use the third-person plural (**ellos/ellas**) form of each verb to create the stem for the imperfect subjunctive. For example:

Take **hablaron**, and remove the **-ron**.

▶ That leaves you with **habla-** to which the **-ra** or **-se** endings are added.

This method of finding the stem for the imperfect subjunctive from the third-person plural of the preterite is valuable when it comes to irregular verbs, so you might as well use it with the regular ones too.

If you find accuracy with verb forms difficult, you do not need to learn the **-se** form of the imperfect subjunctive except to recognize it when you see (or hear) it. The **-ra** form is always possible where the imperfect subjunctive is required, but the **-se** form has other complexities and can sound pretentious in some contexts, so if you decide to live without learning one of the two, miss out the **-se** form.

Fill in the following table with the imperfect subjunctive and underline the stressed vowel:

	hablar	comer	vivir
3rd person plural of the preterite	hablaron	comieron	vivieron]
12 (yo)	hablara	comiera	viviera
13 (tú)	hablaras	comieras	vivieras
14 (él/ella)	hablara	hablaras	viviera
15 (nosotros/-as)	habláramos	comiéramos	viviéramos
16 (vosotros/-as)	_ _ _ _ _ _ _ _	_ _ _ _ _ _ _ _	_ _ _ _ _ _ _ _
17 (ellos/ellas)	hablaron	comieran	vivieran

Practise any other tenses that you think you could be shaky on in the same way – by making a table of the three conjugations.

When you are satisfied that you know all the regular verb forms, try the following:

18 (yo) bailar *to dance* (pres. subj.): baile _

19 (tú) beber *to drink* (imperfect): ~~bebería~~ bebebrás

20 (él) sorprender *to surprise* (preterite): sopprendió

21 (ella) mirar *to look at* (future): mirará

22 (nosotros) pelear *to fight* (pres. indicative): peleamos

23 (vosotros) subir *to go up* (imperf. subj.): _ _ _ _ _ _ _ _ _ _

24 (ellos) discutir *to argue* (pres. perfect): han discutido

25 (ellas) besar *to kiss* (imperfect): besabas

SPOT THE HOWLER!

Below are five of the kind of mistakes that examiners regard as unforgivable. They may be verb forms, agreements, or accents. Read through the piece three times, looking for, and correcting, each type of mistake in turn. Make sure you check your own written Spanish in the same methodical way — reading through several times, each time looking for one specific type of mistake.

---

26 – 30 Juan llego tarde a la escuela aquella mañana. Se fue directamente a sentarse,

esperando que el profesor no le dijera nada. Pero el señor Jiménez no iba a dejarlo

pasar.

- ¿Sabe usted que hora es? - fulminó.

- Sí, señor - respondó Juan con una sonrisa. - Son las diez en punto.

Al profesor no le gustaba que un chico le hablare así delante del resto de la clase.

- ¡Cien líneas! 'Un alumno se disculpe si llega tarde a la escuela.'

Are you still noting down any vocabulary that is new to you as you go along?

Remember that there is little point knowing the infinitive of a verb if you do not know how it is conjugated. So make sure you include that information with each new verb you learn: (a) regular or irregular; (b) if radical-changing, which type it is.

The vocabulary for today is based on the principle introduced in earlier sections, namely, the linking of cognate items: i.e. words that are derived from the same source. But now there will be an opportunity to extend your vocabulary by 'inventing' words that you can guess at. Being able to make a good educated guess is vital to all foreign language learning.

GUESSABILITY

Here you have a chance to practise this skill to help you (a) improve your feel for the sorts of words you are likely to be able to guess right; and (b) see how a knowledge of similar words can contribute to the guessing process. In most cases, an accurate guess is made up of two elements: first, having the knowledge of a cognate term; and second, the knowledge of morphologically similar relationships – that is word-groups with a similar shape. For example, if you wanted to guess the word for 'plum-tree', you would probably get it right if you thought about two things you already know: one, that **la ciruela** means 'plum'; and two, that the names of fruit trees are often formed from the masculine version of the fruit, for example in the pairs **la cereza** [cherry] – **el cerezo** [cherry-tree] and **la naranja** [orange] – **el naranjo** [orange-tree]. That knowledge should lead you to try the word **el ciruelo** for 'plum-tree' – and you will be right. It should also stop you from trying to guess what a lemon-tree is, since you know that **el limón** [lemon] is already masculine, so there is no obvious guess to be made here and this should encourage you to go for a sly paraphrase rather than a rash guess. (A lemon-tree, incidentally, is **un limonero**.)

By the same token, this type of logic combined with previous knowledge should enable you also to work out words from Spanish to English, when you come up against an unfamiliar term. For instance, you would have been able to work out that **el ciruelo** means 'plum tree' if you had already known the words **la ciruela** and **el naranjo**.

Now use this opportunity to practise guessing in the same way.

la fotografía photography
sacar una foto(grafía) to take a photo(graph) (NB the long form is identical to the word for 'photography'. Remember that when you use the short form, **la foto**, the gender looks odd because of the **-o** ending. Finally, note that unexpected verb **sacar**, and that its use extends to photocopies

too: **sacar una fotocopia** to take a photocopy. The **-c** at the end of the stem means it will need some spelling changes – this will be covered on Day 24.)
el/la fotógrafo/a photographer
fotografiar (irreg., cf. **continuar**) to photograph

The use of **foto-** as a prefix is parallel to English, making a host of other words reliably guessable. For example, work out how you say:

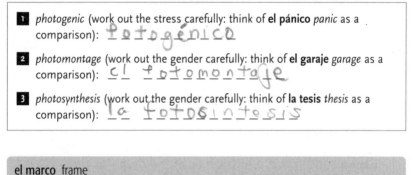

1   *photogenic* (work out the stress carefully: think of **el pánico** *panic* as a comparison): fotogénico

2   *photomontage* (work out the gender carefully: think of **el garaje** *garage* as a comparison): el fotomontaje

3   *photosynthesis* (work out the gender carefully: think of **la tesis** *thesis* as a comparison): la fotosíntesis

---

el marco frame
enmarcar to frame
BUT **marcar** – this is a false friend! It can mean 'to dial' (as in a telephone number), 'to score' (as in a goal), 'to set' (as in one's hair) and, only in certain contexts, 'to mark'

Guess the meaning:

4   **Las negociaciones actuales se enmarcan dentro de la política de diálogo de la cual el gobierno tanto se enorgullece.**

The current negotiations ......are framed around...... *the policy of dialogue of which the government is so proud.*

---

grabar to engrave, also to record (audio or video)   **el grabado** engraving
la grabación recording

Guess the meaning:

5   **La cara de su madre la última vez que la vio se le quedó grabada el resto de su vida.**

For the rest of his life, his mother's face the last time he saw her .... stayed engraved ....

---

cuadrado square (as in geometry), but also squarely or well built (when describing a person)   **un cuadro** picture
el cuadrado the square
BUT **la cuadra** stable

6 Guess how to say *quadraphonic* (think carefully about the likely stress pattern – compare with words like **crónico** *chronic*):

cuadrafónico

---

el agua (fem. – see Day 28 for more on this) water
el aguafuerte etching
una acuarela water-colour (compare with **el acuario** aquarium)

---

7 Guess the Spanish for *water-colourist* (compare with words like **el/la pianista**):

el/la *acuarelista*

---

la escultura sculpture   **el escultor/la escultora** sculptor

---

8 Guess what the verb *to sculpt* would be: *escultar*

---

el esbozo sketch   **esbozar** to sketch

---

9 Guess what you are doing if **esbozas una sonrisa** (and the answer is not drawing a sketch of someone's smile!)

.... *hint of a smile* ....

---

el pincel (false friend: not 'pencil') paintbrush

Guess the meaning:

10 **Este estilo de pintura deja ver las pinceladas.**

This style of painting lets the .... strokes .... show.

---

el cincel chisel

---

11 Guess the verb *to chisel*: *cincelar*

el retrato portrait
retratar to make a portrait of (including photographic)

---

12 Guess *portrait painter* or *photographer* (think of **pianista** again):

el/la _retratista_

Miscellaneous unguessables

el lienzo canvas (for painting) – (for other types of canvas, e.g. for a tent, use other terms)
la pinacoteca art gallery
en primer plano in the foreground

Visita a la pinacoteca

---

13 Can you guess what **un primer plano** would be in photography?

a close-up

COLOURS

Do you know your colours? You probably do, but have you used them as a building block to widen your vocabulary? Here are some ideas; plenty more could be taken from any good dictionary.

blanco y negro black and white (note the reverse order of the colours)
la blancura whiteness

---

14 Guess *blackness*: _la negrura_

blanquear to bleach
blanquecino whitish

rojizo reddish
enrojecerse to blush, turn red (with anger or embarrassment, shame, etc.)

ennegrecer to blacken
negruzco blackish

amarillento yellowish/yellowed (as as in the pages of an old book)
amarillear to yellow/to turn yellow

---

15 Guess the meaning of **grisáceo**: ...... *greyish* ....

---

azulado bluish
el azulejo ceramic tile (for walls) – traditionally featuring the colour blue

---

16 Guess the meaning of **verdoso**: ...... *greenish* ....
17 Guess the meaning of **verdear**: ...... *to green* ....

---

un viejo verde a dirty old man

Now here are a few rarer colours. Why not learn them and then upgrade your written Spanish by deciding to make a point of using one or more of them in describing someone's clothes, the wallpaper of a house, the cover of a book, or whatever else you want?

carmesí (plural: **carmesíes**) crimson
escarlata scarlet
malva mauve
turquesa turquoise
caqui khaki

pardo greyish brown, dun-coloured (a common landscape colour in Castile, hence rather less rare in Spanish than in English)

WORDSEARCH

Find thirteen of today's words written either horizontally (left to right only), or vertically (downwards only), in the following grid. Once you have found them, copy them into the alphabetical list underneath, along with their English translation. Don't forget to include articles with nouns.

B	E	A	C	U	A	R	E	L	A	R	G
L	N	P	I	G	R	A	B	A	D	O	Y
A	M	I	F	G	C	J	E	H	D	J	R
N	A	N	E	G	R	U	Z	C	O	I	P
Q	R	A	L	M	A	L	V	A	S	Z	A
U	C	C	I	R	T	B	S	A	F	O	R
E	A	O	E	S	B	O	Z	A	R	L	D
A	R	T	N	F	Y	I	G	U	E	T	O
R	Z	E	Z	C	A	Q	U	I	T	U	I
E	C	C	O	R	E	T	R	A	T	O	T
L	A	A	Y	J	F	D	E	S	H	J	I

18 _ _   _ _ _ _ _ _ _ _
....

19 _ _ _ _ _ _ _ _
....

20 _ _ _ _ _
....

21 _ _ _ _ _ _ _
....

22 _ _ _ _ _ _
....

23 _ _   _ _ _ _ _ _
....

24 _ _   _ _ _ _ _ _
....

25 _ _ _ _ _
....

26 _ _ _ _ _ _ _ _
....

27 _ _ _ _ _
....

28 _ _   _ _ _ _ _ _ _ _ _ _
....

29 _ _   _ _ _ _ _ _ _
....

30 _ _ _ _ _ _
....

Stop losing marks for accents!
Part II: Overriding stress accents

Are you one of many students who puts an accent on a word 'because it looks right'? If so, face it now: that is not a reliable guideline. If you put your mind to it today, you will be able to use accents confidently and correctly from now on. You have already mastered their use for reasons other than the stress rules. Today we will cover the use of accents as what we might call a 'pronunciation override signal'.

THE IMPORTANCE OF STRESS PATTERNS

Spanish is a language which, like English, gives importance to where the stress falls in the pronunciation of each word. If the stress is placed on the wrong syllable of a word in either Spanish or English it will sound peculiar and maybe incomprehensible. But in Spanish, even more commonly than in English, a change of stress can actually change the meaning. For example:

Spanish: **ha̱blo** [I speak]
           habló̱ [he/she spoke]

English: e̱xport – noun
           expo̱rt – verb

Listen to a learner of English who is hard to understand. You will find the reason will often be that the stress patterns are all wrong, as much as poor pronunciation of certain sounds. It is worth remembering this because it means that learners of Spanish, whose first language is English, *can* hear the difference between stressing one syllable or another, while Francophones, for example, have a much harder time.

Written accents are used in Spanish to indicate where the stress falls on words that do not obey the normal rules of pronunciation (see Day 4 for the other uses). Therefore, if you know those rules and you know how to pronounce a word, you can work out whether it will need an accent or not. By the same token, if you do not know a word that you see written down, you can work out how to pronounce it. That is why it is of paramount importance when you first learn a new word to pronounce it correctly to yourself so that later, when you retrieve it from your memory, you can work out how to spell it.

SEVEN RULES CONCERNING STRESS ACCENTS

You probably already know the two basic rules.

I   **Words ending in a vowel, n, or s** are naturally stressed on the penultimate syllable (Spanish linguists call this stress pattern **llano**). For example:

Barcelo̱na   ha̱blan [they speak]   Ca̱rlos

If a word with one of these endings is stressed anywhere else, it requires a written accent to alert the reader to this fact and override the normal rule. For example:

América	catalán
Bogotá	París

II **Words ending in a consonant** other than **n** or **s** are naturally stressed on the final syllable (Spanish linguists call this stress pattern **agudo**). For example:

Madr<u>i</u>d	González
Isra<u>e</u>l	el fútbol [football]
Cádiz	cap<u>az</u> [capable]

It follows from the above rules that all words that are stressed on the third from last syllable will require an accent; Spanish linguists call these **esdrújulas** – but there is no need to single them out for spelling purposes. For example:

Córdoba	Málaga

Make sure that you are happy thus far by checking the following words for accents. They may be correct as they stand, or need an accent added, or removed, or moved elsewhere in the same word. If they are right, just tick them; if wrong, copy them out corrected. The stressed vowel is underlined to help you.

> **1** **ridiculo** *ridiculous*: _ _ _ _ _ _ _ _
>
> **2** **dijó** *he/she said*: _ _ _ _
>
> **3** **Caracas**: _ _ _ _ _ _ _
>
> **4** **hablarón** *they spoke*: _ _ _ _ _ _ _ _ _
>
> **5** **enórme** *enormous*: _ _ _ _ _ _
>
> **6** **electricidad** *electricity*: _ _ _ _ _ _ _ _ _ _ _ _
>
> **7** **analísis** *analysis*: _ _ _ _ _ _ _ _

Most students find clusters of vowels the hardest. Here are the rules that apply to these cases, but remember the ones practised above go on applying at the same time.

III **Vowels are classified as 'strong' or 'weak'.** The strong vowels are: **a**, **e**, and **o**. The weak vowels are **i** and **u**. If you find this hard to memorize, try a mnemonic such as: <u>a</u>nimals like <u>e</u>lephants and <u>o</u>striches are strong; <u>i</u>nsects are <u>u</u>gly and weak.

IV **Two strong vowels together** are counted as separate syllables. For example:

▶ **europeo** (e + o = 2 separate syllables, so the underlined **e** is the penultimate syllable of the word and as **europeo** ends in a vowel, and the stress falls on that **e**, it obeys rule I above – hence, no accent is required)

▶ **Mediterráneo** (here the stress is falling on the third syllable from last, which does not follow the normal rule, hence the accent)

V **One strong vowel plus one weak vowel** – whichever way round – count as one syllable and if this is the one where the stress of the whole word falls, it will be on the strong vowel. For example:

▶ **Mari̲ano** (i + a = 1 syllable, which is the stressed one of the word because it ends in a vowel and the **ia** are in the penultimate position. The stress falls on **a** which is the strong one; hence it obeys the rules and so has no accent.)

▶ **Val̲encia** (i + a = 1 syllable, which is not the stressed one of the word, because Valencia ends in a vowel. So the stress falls on the penultimate syllable. Rules are all obeyed here, so no accent is required.)

If the stress falls on the weak vowel in a strong + weak combination, an accent will be needed to indicate this. For example:

país, países [country, countries]   **día, días** [day, days]

Note that pluralizing these words will not affect their need for an accent, since it depends on the stress within the vowel combination and not the number of syllables of the word as a whole.

VI **Two weak vowels make one syllable**, naturally stressed on the second of the two, whichever that happens to be. For example:

ru̲ido [noise]   **conclu̲ir** [to conclude]   **vi̲udo** [widower]

Check the accents on the following words, which contain vowel clusters. As before, accents may be correct, missing, superfluous, or on the wrong vowel.

8	**Bilbao** _ _ _ _ _ _
9	**Dolóres** _ _ _ _ _ _ _
10	**dólares** *dollars* _ _ _ _ _ _ _
11	**familia** *family* _ _ _ _ _ _ _
12	**baúles** *trunks* _ _ _ _ _ _
13	**oido** *heard* _ _ _ _
14	**búitre** *vulture* _ _ _ _ _ _
15	**cruél** *cruel* _ _ _ _ _
16	**veintidos** *twenty-two* _ _ _ _ _ _ _ _ _

VII **Irritating but true!** Here are the two anomalous rules of the use of accents for stress.

(i) When an adverb is made from an adjective that has an accent on it, the accent is retained even though a new stress on the first **e** of the **-mente** ending has been added. For example:

> **rápido** [quick] — (adjective)
> **rápidam<u>e</u>nte** [quickly] — (adverb)

(There will be more on adverbs on Day 28.)

(ii) When there is an **h** separating two vowels, it is disregarded, so that the vowels are treated as a cluster. For example:

> **el búho** [owl] has an accent because it is treated as if it were spelt 'búo'. In other words, it is considered as a weak + strong combination. This would mean that the normal stress would be on the strong vowel (**o**). Since it is not, it takes an accent on the weak vowel, (**u**).

Make the following nouns plural, changing the accents as required:

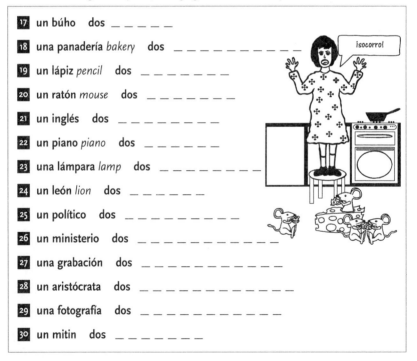

17 un búho   dos _ _ _ _ _

18 una panadería *bakery*   dos _ _ _ _ _ _ _ _ _ _ _   ¡socorro!

19 un lápiz *pencil*   dos _ _ _ _ _ _ _ _

20 un ratón *mouse*   dos _ _ _ _ _ _ _

21 un inglés   dos _ _ _ _ _ _ _

22 un piano *piano*   dos _ _ _ _ _ _

23 una lámpara *lamp*   dos _ _ _ _ _ _ _ _

24 un león *lion*   dos _ _ _ _ _ _

25 un político   dos _ _ _ _ _ _ _ _ _

26 un ministerio   dos _ _ _ _ _ _ _ _ _ _

27 una grabación   dos _ _ _ _ _ _ _ _ _ _ _

28 un aristócrata   dos _ _ _ _ _ _ _ _ _ _ _

29 una fotografía   dos _ _ _ _ _ _ _ _ _ _ _

30 un mitin   dos _ _ _ _ _ _ _

Need extra practice?

If you are weak on accents, try copying out any passage from any Spanish book and leaving off all the accents. Tomorrow, see if you can put them back on correctly. However, you will not gain from this or any other type of practice unless you use the rules explained above.

If you are still depending on what looks right, you are wasting your time. So make sure you maximize the benefits of practice by working with the rules. If you are struggling, start by referring to them as you work and only when you think you have memorized them, test yourself by practising from memory.

Remember that the seven rules above are far less to absorb than the spelling of every individual Spanish word you know!

Have you got the vocabulary you need to talk about literature? Are you one of the many students who tries to avoid reading literary criticism in Spanish because the vocabulary seems daunting? Some of it of course overlaps with general descriptive language, so that what you learnt on Day 2, for example, about describing people, will be just as useful when describing literary characters. Other terms are used not only for literature but in the arts generally and so will complement the vocabulary you learnt on Day 7 for the visual arts.

USING COGNATE TERMS

The vocabulary for today will, as before, group cognate terms and encourage you to guess intelligently as a language-learning strategy. The first group is connected with narrative.

When you think you have learnt the words and phrases below, try the gap-filling exercise that follows.

la **narrativa** narrative
narrar to narrate, tell (of a story)
la **narración** story
el/la **narrador/-ora** narrator, storyteller

el **capítulo** chapter (of book or of monks)
capitular to surrender, capitulate
recapitular to recap(itulate), sum up

la **página** page
volver (irreg. – see Day 19) **la página** to turn over/turn the page
compaginar con to match, to fit in with

el **desenlace** denouement
el **lazo** tie (in sense of attachment, e.g. **lazos familiales** family ties; not the neck garment), also shoelace
enlazar con to connect, link up with

el **argumento** plot, argument (meaning a line of argument, but not a quarrel)
argumentar to argue (meaning 'to reason', not 'to quarrel')

el **epílogo** epilogue

---

1 Guess *monologue*: _ _ _ _ _ _ _ _ _ _

2 Guess *dialogue*: _ _ _ _ _ _ _ _ _

la persona person
el personaje character (in story),
    important person (in real life)
la personificación personification
el personal personnel

la moraleja moral (of story)
la moral morality, morale
inmoral immoral (Notice how the 'imm'
    in English becomes 'inm' in Spanish.
    This is very common and should help
    you guess intelligently. Think, for
    example of inmediatamente
    immediately, or inmaculado
    immaculate)

el/la protagonista protagonist
protagonizar to star, be the main
    character, take the leading role
la agonía death-throes (NB false friend –
    not 'agony' in the common English
    meaning of severe pain)
agonizante dying

el cuento short story
el descuento discount
contar to tell (a story), to recount, to
    count; note how it is possible to
    guess that the verb contar will be
    radical-changing, based on the
    associated nouns (see Day 15 for
    more on this)

Complete the word or phrase, based on the definition:

3 *(male) narrator*: **el** _ _ _ _ _ **dor**

4 *denouement*: **el des** _ _ _ _ _ _

5 *moral (of story)*: **la moral** _ _ _

6 *dying*: _ _ _ _ _ **zante**

7 *to turn over (a page)*: _ _ _ _ _ _ **la página**

8 *plot (e.g. of novel)*: **el** _ _ _ _ **mento**

9 *character (in story)*: **el** _ _ _ _ _ _ **aje**

The second group of vocabulary today is related to poetry:

la poesía poetry, also poem
el poema poem
la poética poetics
poético poetic
el/la poeta poet
la poetisa woman poet (slightly old-
    fashioned)

la rima rhyme (Note that gender does
    not conform to -ma typically
    masculine words like el poema
    above)

10 Guess *to rhyme with*: _ _ _ _ _   _ _ _

Technical terms seem complicated but they are often the easiest to guess. Try these:

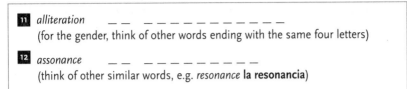

11 *alliteration* _ _ _ _ _ _ _ _ _ _ _ _ _ _
(for the gender, think of other words ending with the same four letters)

12 *assonance* _ _ _ _ _ _ _ _ _ _ _
(think of other similar words, e.g. *resonance* **la resonancia**)

Some terms are hard to guess from English to Spanish, but can easily be recognized. For example, guess the meaning of:

13 **la onomatopeya** ....

14 **onomatopéyico** ....

el ritmo rhythm

15 Guess *rhythmic:* _ _ _ _ _ _ _ _ (for the stress, think of other adjectives with the same ending, e.g. **público** *public,* **anárquico** *anarchic,* **físico** *physical*)

componer (irreg., as **poner** – see Day 19) to compose, to write (a poem or similar)

el/la compositor/-ora composer (of music)

16 Guess *composition:* _ _ _ _ _ _ _ _ _ _ _ _ _ _
(to get the gender and stress right, compare with *alliteration* above)

la sílaba syllable   **silábico** syllabic

17 Guess the meaning of **el octosílabo:** ....

18 Guess the meaning of **el endecasílabo:** ....

(but note the switch of gender and ending of these two relative to **la sílaba**)

el símbolo symbol

> **19** Guess *symbolism*: _ _   _ _ _ _ _ _ _ _ _ _
>
> **20** Guess *symbolist*: _ _ _ _ _ _ _ _ _ _
>
> **21** Guess *symbolic*: _ _ _ _ _ _ _ _ _

el surrealismo surrealism

> **22** Guess *surrealist*: _ _ _ _ _ _ _ _ _ _ _

(*Note* that this is just an example to show you how easy it usually is to translate the names of literary movements. You can probably think of others that fit the same **-ismo, -ista** pattern, such as **el realismo** and **realista**.)

One miscellaneous loner:

la estrofa stanza, verse (when it means 'stanza')

The last vocabulary group relates to drama.

la comedia drama (not 'comedy' in the common English sense of 'humour')

la comedia musical musical

el/la comediante/-ta actor/actress (slightly old-fashioned, rather like saying 'player' for 'actor' in English)

el/la cómico/-a comedian/comedienne, comic actor/actress (false friend – it does not mean 'a comic' for children)

la tragicomedia tragicomedy

hacer mutis to exit
mudo mute, dumb

el soliloquio soliloquy
locuaz talkative
la locución phrase
el/la ventrílocuo/-a ventriloquist

la escena scene
el escenario stage (a false friend – it does not mean 'scenario')
en escena on stage

los bastidores wings
entre bastidores offstage, behind the scenes
el bastidor embroidery frame

el papel role, paper
hacer el papel de . . . to play the part of . . .
la papelera waste paper basket
el papeleo red tape

el drama drama
el/la dramaturgo/-a dramatist, playwright
el melodrama melodrama
dramatizar to (over)dramatize

el teatro theatre
la obra de teatro play
teatral theatrical

el estreno opening night
estrenar to open (of play), to wear or use for the first time
estrenarse to make one's debut

representar to perform, represent
la representación performance, representation, representative office (as in **este banco tiene una representación en Londres**)
el/la representante representative (not performer)

CROSSWORD

The crossword contains vocabulary taken from the second and third of the vocabulary lists for today. As you fill in the grid, try to remember as many as you can of the other cognate words in the vocabulary lists above, and write them out with their meanings underneath.

23 – 30 The complete and correct answer to each of the clues is worth half a point:

ACROSS

1. *The musical* (2,7,7) + 4 related terms and their meanings:

   _ _ _ _ _ _ _ _ _ _ _ _ _ _ _ _ ....

   el/la _ _ _ _ _ _ _ _ _ _ _ /-ta ....

   el/la _ _ _ _ _ _ /-a ....

   _ _ _ _ _ _ _ _ _ _ _ _ _ ....

3. *To exit* (5,5) + 1 related term and its meaning

   _ _ _ _ ....

6. *Red tape* (2,7) + 3 related terms and their meanings

   _ _ _ _ _ _ _ _ ....

   _ _ _ _ _ _ _ _ _ _ _ _ _ _ ....

   _ _ _ _ _ _ _ _ _ _ ....

8. *Behind the scenes* (5,10) + 2 related terms and their meanings

   _ _ _ _ _ _ _ _ _ _ _ _ _ ....

   _ _ _ _ _ _ _ _ _ _ ....

11. *Syllable* (2,6) + 3 related terms and their meanings

   _ _ _ _ _ _ _ ....

   _ _ _ _ _ _ _ _ _ _ _ _ ....

   _ _ _ _ _ _ _ _ _ _ _ _ _ ....

12. *Playwright* (male) (2,10) + 3 related terms and their meanings

   _ _ _ _ _ _ _ ....

   _ _ _ _ _ _ _ _ _ _ _ ....

   _ _ _ _ _ _ _ _ _ ....

15. *Drama* (2,7) – one of the related terms from 1 across.

DOWN

1. *Talkative* (6) + 3 related terms and their meanings

    — — — — — — — — — — —   ....

    — — — — — — — — —   ....

    el/la _ _ _ _ _ _ _ _ _ _ _/**-a**   ....

2. *Stage* (2,9) + 2 related terms and their meanings

    — — — — — — —   ....

    — — — — — — —   ....

4. *To perform* (11) + 2 related terms and their meanings

    — — — — — — — — — — — — —   ....

    el/la _ _ _ _ _ _ _ _ _ _ _ _   ....

5. Singular definite article for **rima** + 1 related term and its meaning

    — — — — — — —   ....

7. *Theatrical* (7) + 2 related terms and their meanings

    — — — — — — —   ....

    — — — — — — — — — — — — —   ....

9. *To wear for the first time* (8) + 2 related terms and their meanings

    — — — — — — — —   ....

    — — — — — — — —   ....

10. *Poem* (2,5) + 5 related terms and their meanings

    — — — — — — —   ....

    — — — — — — — —   ....

    — — — — — —   ....

    el/la _ _ _ _ _   ....

    — — — — — — —   ....

13. *mute* (4) – related term from 3 across.

14. Singular definite article for *melodrama* (2) – one of the related terms from 12 across.

Easier than you think:
ser and *estar*

It is not as difficult as you might think to make the right choice between ser *and* estar. *Some of the distinctions – and teachers love them because they lead to interesting classroom discussion and exercises – are tricky or subtle. But you can avoid most problem situations with a little ingenuity coupled with a sound command of the basics. Today's exercises will therefore concentrate on those two strategies: one, knowing the basics; and two, avoiding the problem cases altogether.*

USES OF *SER* AND *ESTAR*
In some ways the permanent (**ser**) versus temporary (**estar**) distinction that most students are taught is only of limited use. You will see some common examples of these limitations below and you may know of others. Here are some additional points that might help.

I Ser
Ser must be used whenever there is a noun complement. That means, whenever one is saying x is someone or something, the verb 'to be' will have to be **ser**. For example:

> **Mi padre es abogado** (noun complement); **de joven quería ser pianista** (noun complement), **pero así es la vida** (noun complement). **Desde hace dos años es viudo** (noun complement).
> [My father is a lawyer; in his youth he wanted to be a pianist, but such is life. He has been a widower for two years.]

Note that even if the noun complement alludes to a temporary condition, you cannot even consider using **estar**. The father may still be a pianist at heart even though he became a lawyer and he has not always been a widower, nor may remain one for long, but none of this is relevant simply because the grammatical noun complement rule demands **ser**.

II Estar
Estar must be used for location (it derives from the Latin verb meaning 'to stand'). Contrast these two sentences:

> **Caracas está en Venezuela.** [Caracas is in Venezuela.]
> **Caracas es la capital de Venezuela.** [Caracas is the capital of Venezuela.]

In the first, **estar** is obligatory because we are talking about location (even though Caracas is not about to move and so you might easily want to argue that it is permanently in Venezuela). In the second, **ser** is obligatory because of the noun complement: 'capital'.

III Estar + the continuous
Estar must be used for the continuous tenses. **Ser** cannot even be considered.

Estoy hablando. [I am speaking.]

IV Ser and Estar + adjective
The hardest cases are often when 'to be' is followed by an adjective, because then both **ser** and **estar** are grammatically possible and the meaning has to be considered in order to make the right choice. Remember the link between **estar** and **estado** (state) and ask yourself if a state is what is being described. For example, look at these three sentences:

La hierba es verde. [Grass is green.]

La hierba estaba blanqueada por el sol. [The grass was bleached by the sun.]

No hay que comer un plátano si está verde, porque no está maduro.
[One should not eat a banana if it is green, because it is not ripe.]

In the first, **ser** is used because the sentence is not talking about the state of the grass but its natural colour, an inherent quality. In the second, the grass is in a particular state – sun-bleached – at a particular time, so **estar** is the right choice. In the third, the greenness of the banana relates to its unripe state, hence **estar** is the right choice both times in the sentence.

These are fairly clear-cut cases, but they are not always so obvious, and when you are faced with a problematic decision, see if you can avoid having to make it altogether by using a different verb or a different construction. It may well make your Spanish more natural-sounding into the bargain! Here are a few ideas.

ALTERNATIVES
V Quedar
Try **quedar** instead. For example: for surprise and related conditions:

Este jersey me queda ancho

Me quedé asombrado al oír decir que se habían casado. [I was astonished to hear that they had got married.]

Sometimes **quedar** is the usual and best choice for an expression which in English would use the verb 'to be'. For example:

Este jersey me queda ancho. [This jumper is big for me.]

VI Andar
Try **andar** instead. For example, to talk about health, **estar** is often an easy choice: ¿cómo **estás?** is taught in most students' very first Spanish lesson. But imagine you began to worry

because you were talking about the health of a permanent invalid. Why not avoid the issue altogether? For example:

No anda bien de salud mi hermano, el pobre, como siempre.
[My brother is not in good health, poor thing, as usual.]

Another example:

No me gusta andar sin dinero encima. [I don't like to be without money on me.]

VII **tener** + noun
Change an English construction of 'to be + adjective' to a Spanish construction: '**tener** + noun'. You already know the obligatory ones, such as **tener hambre / sed / frío / calor** etc. [to be hungry / thirsty / cold / hot].
Remember that you can use this strategy as an option to avoid a **ser / estar** debate. For example, for 'to be popular':

Ese cantante tiene gran popularidad en Estados Unidos. [That singer is very popular in the USA.]

and for 'to be reputed to be s.th.':

Este dramaturgo tiene fama de mujeriego. [This playwright is reputed to be a womanizer.]

Change your sentence round so that another verb altogether can be used. This is especially useful with constructions in English that are 'to be + past participle', such as 'to be admired'. Since **ser** is used for the passive, but **estar** can also be used with a past participle to denote a state, the choice can be troublesome, so avoid it if you are in any doubt. For example:

Se le conoce en España, pero no en Inglaterra.
[He is known in Spain, but not in England.]

In the following sentences, ring the correct verb:

1 **A mi hijo le gusta hacer el ganso: es / está un auténtico payaso; a lo mejor se le pasará con la edad.**
My son likes playing the fool: he's a real clown; he'll probably grow out of it.

2 **Barcelona es / está la ciudad más importante de Cataluña.**
Barcelona is the largest city in Catalunya.

3 **Cuando sonó el teléfono, era / estaba durmiendo.**
When the telephone rang, I was asleep.

4, **5** **Los gatos son / están animales fáciles de cuidar pero los perros son / están más fieles.**
Cats are easy to look after, but dogs are more faithful animals.

In the next exercise, fill the gaps with a construction that avoids the use of **ser** or **estar**. Make sure you use the right tense and mood. The infinitive of the constructions is given below in alphabetical order to help you; each one will be used once.

> **andar corto de** to be short of . . .
> **dar pánico** to make one panic, fill one with dread
> **enfurecer** to infuriate
> **quedar estrecho** to be small for
> **quedarse horrorizado** to be horrified
> **tener ganas de** to be in the mood to . . .

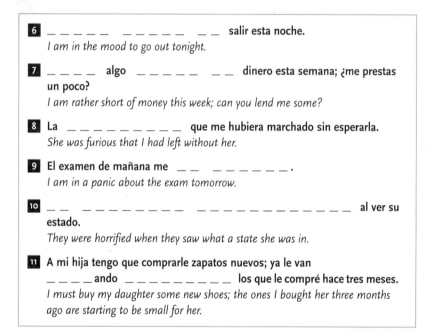

6 _ _ _ _ _   _ _ _ _ _   _ _ salir esta noche.
I am in the mood to go out tonight.

7 _ _ _ _ _ algo _ _ _ _ _   _ _ dinero esta semana; ¿me prestas un poco?
I am rather short of money this week; can you lend me some?

8 La _ _ _ _ _ _ _ _ _ _ que me hubiera marchado sin esperarla.
She was furious that I had left without her.

9 El examen de mañana me _ _   _ _ _ _ _ _ _.
I am in a panic about the exam tomorrow.

10 _ _   _ _ _ _ _ _ _ _ _   _ _ _ _ _ _ _ _ _ _ _ _ al ver su estado.
They were horrified when they saw what a state she was in.

11 A mi hija tengo que comprarle zapatos nuevos; ya le van _ _ _ _ _ando _ _ _ _ _ _ _ _ _ _ los que le compré hace tres meses.
I must buy my daughter some new shoes; the ones I bought her three months ago are starting to be small for her.

Here are ten set expressions with **estar**. The first is a classic example of the limited usefulness of the 'permanent' versus 'temporary' idea. Memorizing them will help you in two ways: first it will guarantee that you get the right verb 'to be' for these common cases; second, it should help you acquire a feel for the use of **estar** that will allow you to choose correctly when other expressions are needed.

> **estar muerto** to be dead (rather permanent! – but still a state)
> **estar vivo** to be alive
> **estar cansado** to be tired
> **estar enfermo** to be ill (even if condition is chronic)
> **estar listo** to be ready
> **estar guapo** to look attractive
> **estar enfadado** to be angry
> **estar contento** to be pleased
> **estar solo** to be alone
> **estar loco** to be mad (even if incurable)

Now here are nine expressions for **ser**, to memorize for the same reasons as those for **estar**. *Note* the first two are flagrant contradictions of the temporary/permanent distinction.

ser joven to be young (not at all permanent, unfortunately!)	**ser listo** to be clever
	ser tonto to be foolish
ser viejo to be old	**ser guapo** to be attractive
ser español (or any other nationality or regional origin) to be Spanish (even though one may lose or acquire nationality through emigration)	**ser feliz** to be (profoundly) happy
	ser egoísta to be selfish
	ser aburrido to be boring

Fill the gaps with an appropriate choice from the two lists above. Each expression will be used once.

12 ¡Qué _ _ _ _ _   _ _ _ _ _ con ese vestido!
You look great in that dress!

13 Mi abuelo nació en Rusia pero de nacionalidad _ _ _ _ _ _ _ _ _ .
My grandfather was born in Russia but he is of Spanish nationality.

14 Cuando _ _ _ _ _ _   _ _ _ _ _ _ _ , nos gustaba reunirnos en este bar.
When we were young, we used to like to get together in this bar.

15 _ _ _ _ _   _ _ _ _ _ _ _ _ de verte después de tanto tiempo.
I am glad to see you after such a long time.

16 ¿Te da miedo esa araña pequeña? Pero, ¡qué _ _ _ _ _   _ _ _ _!
Are you scared of that little spider? You are silly!

17 Cuando _ _ _ _ _ _   _ _ _ _ _ llámame por teléfono e iré a buscarte en seguida.
When you're ready, phone me and I'll come and fetch you straight away.

18 ¿ _ _ _ _ _   _ _ _ _ ? Necesito hablarte de un asunto personal.
Are you alone? I need to talk to you about a personal matter.

19 ¡Cuánto te quiero! _ _ _ _ _   _ _ _ _ _ _ _ , ¿verdad?
I love you so much! We are happy, aren't we?

20, **21** Se decía que las dos hermanas _ _ _ _   _ _ _ _ _ _ _ , pero Dolores _ _ _ más _ _ _ _ _ que Amparo.
People used to say that the two sisters were pretty, but Dolores was prettier than Amparo.

22 Juan se arregla siempre para tener más que comer que el resto de la
familia: _ _ un chico muy _ _ _ _ _ _ _ _.
*Juan always manages to get more to eat than the rest of the family; he is a
very selfish boy.*

23 Cuando llegó la ambulancia al hospital el pobre hombre ya _ _ _ _ _ _
_ _ _ _ _ _.
When the ambulance reached the hospital the poor man was already dead.

24, 25 Cuando _ _ _ _ _ _ _ _, le gustaba pasar horas enteras en el
parque, dando de comer a los patos. Luego, cuando _ _ _ _ _ _
_ _ _ _ _ _ _, volvía a casa a descansar.
*When he was old, he used to enjoy spending hours and hours at the park,
feeding the ducks. Then, when he was tired, he would go home for a rest.*

26 ¿No piensas salir vestido así? Pero, ¡si _ _ _ _ _ _ _ _ _ _!
You're not planning to go out dressed like that? You're mad!

27 No te recomiendo este libro; _ _ bastante _ _ _ _ _ _ _ _ _.
I don't recommend this book; it's quite boring.

28 A pesar de haber pasado tres días atrapados debajo de los escombros
del edificio, un niño y a una mujer _ _ _ _ _ _ _ _ _ _ _ _
cuando el equipo de socorro logró sacarles.
*Despite having spent three days trapped underneath the remains of the
building, a child and a woman were alive when the rescue team managed to
pull them out.*

29 Su padre _ _ _ _ _ _ _ _ _ _ _ _ _ _ con ella porque
había salido sin su permiso.
*Her father was angry with her because she had gone out without his
permission.*

30 Ahora tengo una salud de roble, pero de pequeña _ _ _ _ _ _ todo
el tiempo _ _ _ _ _ _ _ _.
*I have a cast-iron constitution now, but when I was a child I was ill the
whole time.*

You will improve both the accuracy and the style of your Spanish if you look out when you are reading and observe not only how **ser** and **estar** are used, but also what other verbs and constructions can replace the use of either of them. This section has only scratched the surface of the alternatives; see how many more you can spot when you read and keep a section in your notes especially for these constructions.

Geographical vocabulary is as useful for narrative purposes as it is for non-fictional contexts. This first set of word-groups relates to physical geography.

el mapa map (note the gender)
el mapamundi map of the world
el mapa político political map (but also used figuratively for political landscape)

la sierra mountain range, saw (think of its serrated edge)
serrar to saw (notice how the radical change is guessable from the noun, sierra – see Day 15)
el serrín sawdust
serrano from or of the mountains as in **el jamón serrano** Spanish ham, rather like Parma ham, originally a mountain speciality

las estribaciones foothills
estribar en to stem from
el estribo stirrup

el norte north
el norteño northerner
hacia el norte north(wards)
sin norte directionless, aimless (Think of not having a compass to show you which way is north.)
el noreste northeast
el noroeste northwest
del norte BUT ALSO **septentrional** northern

el sur south
el sureño southerner
hacia el sur south(wards)
del sur BUT ALSO **meridional, austral** southern
el mediodía the south (like the French *le midi*)
sud- prefix for south, e.g. **Sudáfrica** South Africa
el sudeste (or **sureste**) southeast
el sudoeste (or **suroeste**) southwest

el este, el oriente the east, the orient BUT ALSO **el Levante** (esp. of Spain); think of the sun rising in the east
del este, oriental eastern, oriental
hacia el este east(wards)
el oeste, el occidente the west, the occident
del oeste, occidental western
hacia el oeste west(wards)

la costa coast
costero coastal
el costeño s.o. who lives on coast

el río river
la riada flood
la ribera riverbank or shore of lake
el ribereño s.o. who lives by a river or lake

A few miscellaneous, but useful items:
el litoral coast(line)
la colina hill
la meseta plateau (think of a flat table top)
el valle valley (note gender differs from French)

Fill in the gaps with an appropriate choice from the lists above. Each expression is used once.

1 – **2**   De joven, vivía en una casita situada en _ _ _
_ _ _ _ _ _ _ _ _ _ _ _ _ _ de la _ _ _ _ _ _ Nevada.
In my youth, I lived in a little house in the foothills of the Sierra Nevada mountains.

3   Después del espectáculo, la gente salió del teatro en _ _ _ _ _ _ _.
After the show, the people flooded out of the theatre.

4   Se ha escrito mucha poesía elogiando la belleza austera de _ _
_ _ _ _ _ _ castellana.
A great deal of poetry has been written in praise of the austere beauty of the Castilian plateau.

5 – **6**   En _ _ _ _ _ _ _ _ _ _ _ , se considera a los estadounidenses
como _ _ _ _ _ _ _ _ _.
In South America, people from the USA are considered 'northerners'.

7   _ _ _ _ _ _ _ _ _ de Inglaterra es la región más rica del
país.
The south-east of England is the richest part of the country.

8   Es una compañía que tiene sucursales en casi todos los países de la
Europa _ _ _ _ _ _ _ _ _ _.
It is a company with branches in almost every Western European country.

9   _ _ _ _ _ _ _ _ _ _ _ _ actual difiere bastante del que
conocíamos hace veinte años.
The present-day world map looks quite different from the one we knew twenty years ago.

10   Los pueblos _ _ _ _ _ _ _ _ _ _ _ _ de Europa tienen un
estilo de vida envidiado por el resto del continente.
The southern Europeans have a lifestyle that is the envy of the rest of the continent.

The following set of word-groups is a very small selection of proper nouns relating to geography. Remember that only place names have initial capitals in Spanish; the adjectives and the nouns denoting the people from the place are not capitalized. The easiest and most common ones (such as **Francia** – f̲rancés) have not been selected to leave space for the slightly trickier or less common – but still useful – ones. If you have an interest in a corner of the world that is not included in the list below, make sure you know the Spanish for all the relevant place names and their adjectives, so that you can talk and write about it happily if the opportunity arises.

París; parisino Paris; Parisian

Burdeos Bordeaux, claret, wine-coloured

Estrasburgo Strasbourg

Londres; londinense London; Londoner

Edimburgo Edinburgh

el país de Gales; galés Wales; Welsh

el Príncipe de Gales Prince of Wales (and Prince of Wales check for a suit)

el condado county

el conde count (title of nobility)

Bélgica; belga Belgium; Belgian

Flandes; flamenco Flanders; Flemish, Fleming, flamingo, flamenco

Brujas Bruges

Lieja Liège

Grecia; griego Greece; Greek

Atenas Athens

los Países Bajos; holandés the Netherlands; Dutch

la holanda fine linen

La Haya the Hague (Note that this is a rare exception to the rule of using a masculine definite article for a feminine word beginning with a stressed 'a' or 'ha', such as **el agua** (fem.) – see Day 28)

Suecia; sueco Sweden; Swedish, Swede (person, not vegetable!)

Estocolmo Stockholm

Dinamarca; danés Denmark; Danish

el Gran Danés Great Dane (dog)

Polonia; polaco Poland; Polish, Pole (person, not geographical)

Varsovia Warsaw

Nueva York; neoyorquino New York; New Yorker

la Nueva Inglaterra New England – and you already know 'Texas' and 'Texan', from Day 2 (think of jeans)

Argelia; argelino Algeria; Algerian (note that reversal of consonants)

Argel Algiers

Marruecos; marroquí (plural: **marroquíes**) Morocco; Moroccan (Note that letter 'a' in Spanish, where English has 'o' – cf. **el tabaco** tobacco)

Tánger Tangiers

Líbano; libanés Lebanon; Lebanese

Venecia; veneciano Venice; Venetian

Florencia; florentino Florence; Florentine

Check you know the above by filling the gaps:

 Una mujer de Suecia es una _ _ _ _ _ . Si es de Marruecos, es una _ _ _ _ _ _ _ _ _ .

A woman from Sweden is a Swede. If she is from Morocco, she is a Moroccan.

13–**14** Nací en Venecia pero mis padres son de Florencia así que no sé si soy
_ _ _ _ _ _ _ _ _ _ o _ _ _ _ _ _ _ _ _ _ .
I was born in Venice but my parents are from Florence, so I don't know if
I'm Venetian or Florentine.

15 Siân es de Cardiff. Es _ _ _ _ _ _ .
Siân is from Cardiff. She is Welsh.

16 La moda _ _ _ _ _ _ _ _ _ me gusta más que la milanesa.
I prefer Paris to Milan fashion.

17–**18** Mis padres son _ _ _ _ _ _ ; mi madre es de Lieja y mi padre de
Brujas; por lo tanto soy bilingüe en francés y _ _ _ _ _ _ _ _ .
My parents are Belgian; my mother is from Liège and my father from
Bruges; therefore I am bilingual in French and Flemish.

19 Los taxistas _ _ _ _ _ _ _ _ _ _ _ _ _ tienen fama de ser los
más groseros del mundo.
New York taxi-drivers are reputed to be the rudest in the world.

20 La capital de Polonia es _ _ _ _ _ _ _ _ .
The capital of Poland is Warsaw.

The last set is concerned with human and urban geography:

la estadística statistic(s) (The singular is
    used in Spanish to denote the subject
    that one might study, but the plural is
    used for a particular set of statistics)
el/la estadístico/-a statistician (Note that
    'female statistician' is the same as the
    word for statistic(s))

el porcentaje percentage
**subir/bajar en un 10% (diez por
    ciento)** to go up/down by 10%
    (Watch that preposition!)

el promedio average
la familia media the average family
sacar (spelling changes needed here –
    see Day 24) **el promedio** to find the
    average
el medio ambiente the environment

la aldea village
el/la aldeano/-a villager

la urbe big city, metropolis
urbano urban, urbane
el urbanismo town planning
la urbanización development (in the
    sense of creating a new built-up area)

el plano street map
el plan plan (in the sense of strategy,
    e.g. **un plan nacional** a national
    programmme)
planificar to plan, make a plan
la planificación familiar family planning

el edificio building
edificar to build, edify
edificante edifying

la población population, BUT ALSO town
el pueblo large village, small town, BUT
    ALSO a people
pueblerino having a small-town
    mentality

la ciudad city	inmigrar to immigrate
el/la ciudadano/-a citizen	el/la inmigrante immigrant
la ciudadanía citizenship	el/la inmigrante económico/-a
la ciudadela citadel	economic migrant
	la inmigración immigration
emigrar to emigrate	
el/la emigrado/-a emigré	
la emigración emigration	

For each of the following single words, provide

a) gender if it is a noun (ring the correct answer)
b) an English translation
c) the number of cognates asked for and their meanings

You score one point for each wholly correct and complete set.

21 **ciudad** a) masc. / fem. b) ....
c) 3 cognates + meaning:

— — — — — — — — — —   ....

— — — — — — — — — — —   ....

— — — — — — — — — — —   ....

22 **población** a) masc. / fem. b) .... and ....
c) 2 cognates + meaning

— — — — — — — —   ....

— — — — — — — — —   ....

23 **medio ambiente** a) masc. / fem. b) ....
c) 3 cognates + meaning

— — — — — — — — — —   ....

— — — — — — — — — — — —   ....

— — — — — — — — — — — — —   ....

24 **aldea** a) masc. / fem. b) ....
c) 1 cognate + meaning

— — — — — — — — —   ....

25 **urbanización** a) masc. / fem. b) ....
c) 3 cognates + meaning

— — — — — —   ....

— — — — — —   .... and ....

— — — — — — — — — —   ....

26 emigración a) masc. / fem. b) ....

  c) 6 cognates + meaning

     _ _ _ _ _ _ _   ....

     el/la _ _ _ _ _ _ _ _ /-a   ....

     _ _ _ _ _ _ _ _   ....

     el/la _ _ _ _ _ _ _ _ _   ....

     el/la _ _ _ _ _ _ _ _ _ _   _ _ _ _ _ _ _ _ _ /-a

     ....

     _ _   _ _ _ _ _ _ _ _ _   ....

27 edificio a) masc. / fem. b) ....

  c) 2 cognates + meaning

     _ _ _ _ _ _ _ _   .... and ....

     _ _ _ _ _ _ _ _ _ _   ....

28 porcentaje a) masc. / fem. b) ....

  c) 1 cognate + meaning

     _ _ _ _ _ / _ _ _ _ _   _ _   _ _   10   _ _ _

     _ _ _ _ _ _   ....

29 plano a) masc. / fem. b) ....

  c) 3 cognates + meaning

     _ _   _ _ _ _   ....

     _ _ _ _ _ _ _ _ _ _   ....

     _ _   _ _ _ _ _ _ _ _ _ _ _ _ _   _ _ _ _ _ _ _

     ....

30 estadística a) masc. / fem. b) ....(s)

  c) 1 cognate + meaning

     el/la _ _ _ _ _ _ _ _ _ _ _ /-a   ....

Make sure you get some credit for knowing this vocabulary. If you have to write in Spanish (or speak in an oral examination), make a point of working some of it in. You can always make one of your characters a New Yorker, or a Parisian, in a narrative piece, for example. You can always anchor the action in a landscape such as **las estribaciones de . . .** and then choose your preferred mountain range: **los Andes, los Pirineos,** etc. In a discursive piece, you may be able to discuss statistics and averages, even if you are not in a specifically geographical context.

Are you one of the many students of Spanish who simply translates directly from English when talking about time? If you are, you will have found that you are often wrong and, at best, not Spanish-sounding. The key to solving this problem is to accept that English expresses time rather differently from Spanish. So the only way to be accurate and natural-sounding is to learn the principal Spanish constructions and their English equivalents off pat. Once you get your mind round the Spanish way of thinking about it, it will become quite easy.

The subtleties of regional variation and other nuances of meaning are not covered here. This is in the interests of providing you with a clear method to upgrade your own Spanish by knowing a straightforward and accurate way of expressing ideas concerned with time, which will be understood and considered correct by all Spanish speakers.

l Time elapsed

In Spanish, there are three basic ways of constructing sentences referring to periods of time elapsed in Spanish. All are equally correct and acceptable, so if you find this difficult, pick on the one you find least muddling to learn actively. For the other two, just make sure you understand them. For example:

> I have been waiting for the bus for an hour.
> I had been waiting for the bus for an hour.

i) First method: using **hace** or **hacía**

> **Hace una hora que espero el autobús.**
> **Hacía una hora que esperaba el autobús.**

ii) Second method: using **desde hace** or **desde hacía**

> **Espero el autobús desde hace una hora.**
> **Esperaba el autobús desde hacía una hora.**

iii) Third method: using **llevar**

> **Llevo una hora esperando el autobús.**
> **Llevaba una hora esperando el autobús.**

Notice how, in all three methods, the Spanish tenses differ from the English in the same way: Spanish is always one tense 'ahead' of the English.

English present perfect	→	Spanish present
[have been waiting]		**hace, espero, llevo**
English pluperfect	→	Spanish imperfect
[had been waiting]		**hacía, esperaba, llevaba**

Fill the gaps in the English translations of the following:

1 **Llevaba dos meses viviendo en España cuando la conocí.**
   I .... *living in Spain for two months when I met her.*

2 **¿Desde hace cuánto tiempo estudias el español?**
   For how long .... *learning Spanish?*

3 **Hace mucho tiempo que está muerto.**
   He .... *a long time.*

II Time past

If time has passed since you last did something, Spanish focuses on the intervening period when you were not doing it, rather than the last occasion when you did, as English often does. For example:

¡Cuánto tiempo sin verte! [What a long time since we saw each other!]

Whereas English thinks back to the last time we saw each other, Spanish refers to the intervening period when we were not seeing each other.

This may occur alongside the three basic types of expression of time that were discussed at the beginning of this section. For example:

We haven't seen each other for a year.
It's been a year since we last saw each other.

We hadn't seen each other for a year.
It had been a year since we had last seen each other.

As these alternative ways of saying the same thing show, in English it is possible to focus either on the intervening period when we were not seeing each other, or on the last time we saw each other before that period began.

In Spanish the basic way of translating either alternative is by focusing on the period when we were not seeing each other.

i) First method:
   Hace un año que no nos vemos.
   Hacía un año que no nos veíamos.

ii) Second method:
   No nos vemos desde hace un año.
   No nos veíamos desde hacía un año.

iii) Third method:

Llevamos un año sin vernos.
Llevábamos un año sin vernos.

It is possible to construct a Spanish sentence that looks back to our last meeting, but it sounds more dramatic than the English sentences above and is more like 'The last time we saw each other was a year ago': **La última vez que nos vimos fue hace un año.** It would be appropriate, for example, if the person you saw a year ago was now dead and you were talking about the last time ever that you saw him/her.

Therefore, it is sensible to stick to the basic principle that for the idea of x time since one last did something, use one of the three methods above and focus on the intervening period.

A maximum of three possible translations are given, with blanks in the key places, for each of the sentences below. Where three are given, they correspond (in order) to the three methods given above. Score one mark for filling at least one in correctly:

---

4 _ _ _ _ _ muchos años que _ _ _ _ _ _ el piano.
_ _ _ _ _ _ el piano _ _ _ _ _ _ _ _ _ _ muchos años.
_ _ _ _ _ _ muchos años _ _ _ _ _ _ _ _ el piano.
I haven't played the piano for many years.

5 _ _ _ _ _ _ varias semanas _ _ _ _ _ _ _ lo viera.
_ _ _ _ _ lo _ _ _ _ desde _ _ _ _ _ varias semanas.
It had been several weeks since anybody had seen him.
(Method 3 is not possible here because of the impersonal form of the sentence – there is no subject for **llevar**.)

6 _ _ _ _ _ un siglo que _ _ _ _ _ _ esto.
_ _ _ _ _ _ esto _ _ _ _ _ _ _ _ _ _ un siglo.
_ _ _ _ _ _ un siglo _ _ _ _ _ _ _ _ esto.
I haven't done this for ages.

7 _ _ _ _ _ _ veinte años al menos _ _ _ _ _ _ _ _ al circo.
_ _ _ _ _ al circo _ _ _ _ _ _ _ _ _ _ _ veinte años al
menos.
_ _ _ _ _ _ _ veinte años al menos _ _ _ _ _ al circo.
She hadn't been to the circus for at least twenty years.

8 _ _ _ _ _ seis años que _ _ _ _ _ _ _ _ español.
_ _ _ _ _ _ _ español _ _ _ _ _ _ _ _ _ _ seis años.
_ _ _ _ _ _ seis años _ _ _ _ _ _ _ _ _ _ _ _ español.
I've been learning Spanish for six years.

III Durante

Use **durante** for a period of time only if:

a)   English would use the word 'during', or

b)   you are referring to the past.

For example:

Lo haremos durante las vacaciones. (Eng. would use 'during')
[We'll do it during the holidays.]

Que nadie me moleste durante mi siesta. (Eng. 'during')
[Don't disturb me during my siesta.]

Estuvo en la cárcel durante cinco años. (not equivalent to 'during', but in the past)
[He was in prison for five years.]

For the future equivalent of this idea of 'for x period of time', you must seek an alternative. The easiest one – altogether avoiding the **por/para** debate – is to change the sentence to one using **pasar**:

Pasará cinco años en la cárcel. [He'll be in prison for five years.]

This is a good way round the problem in general: when you want to say 'for x time' in the future, change the sentence to one using **pasar**.

Try these:

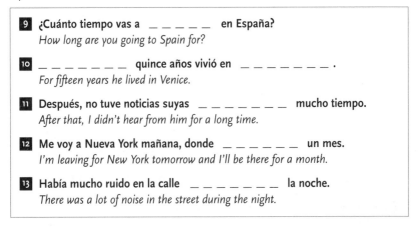

9 ¿Cuánto tiempo vas a _ _ _ _ _ en España?
How long are you going to Spain for?

10 _ _ _ _ _ _ _ _ quince años vivió en _ _ _ _ _ _ _ _ .
For fifteen years he lived in Venice.

11 Después, no tuve noticias suyas _ _ _ _ _ _ _ _ mucho tiempo.
After that, I didn't hear from him for a long time.

12 Me voy a Nueva York mañana, donde _ _ _ _ _ _ un mes.
I'm leaving for New York tomorrow and I'll be there for a month.

13 Había mucho ruido en la calle _ _ _ _ _ _ _ la noche.
There was a lot of noise in the street during the night.

IV Very short periods of time

The simplest way to deal with these is to use nothing or **por**:

por un momento, segundo, instante [for a moment, second, instant]
Por un instante, creí que me volvía loco. [For a moment I thought I was going mad.]
Por un segundo, lo creí muerta. [For a second I thought she was dead.]

It is worth noting that Spanish uses **momento** more than English uses 'moment', so it is often appropriate to translate **momento** by something more common than 'moment'. **Momentito** is often 'hang on' (especially on the telephone). For example:

Ven aquí un momento, ¿quieres? [Come here a minute, could you?]
Espera un momento; ahora vengo. [Wait a second; I'm just coming.]

Notice how English often omits 'for' in these types of case too.

Fill the gaps:

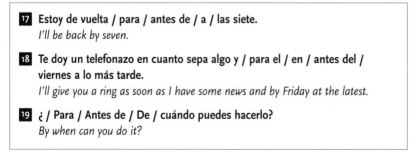

14 **Siéntate** _ _ _ _ _ _ _ _ _ **; estoy casi listo.**
Sit down for a minute; I'm nearly ready.

15 _ _ _ _ _ _ _ _ _ _ **; ahora le paso el Sr. González.**
Hold on; I'm just putting you through to Mr González.

16 _ _ _ _ _ _ _ _ _ _ _ _ **me pareció ridículo todo; luego lo comprendí.**
For a second it all seemed ridiculous and then I understood.

V By a certain time

i) **Para** is the closest to this English idea. For example:

I have to be there by ten o'clock.
Tengo que estar allí para las diez.
(Spanish implies that if I arrive at exactly ten o'clock, I am not too late.)

ii) When the important point is to be in a certain place before the time mentioned, use **antes de**. For example:

This piece of work must be handed in by 4 o'clock on Friday afternoon.
Este trabajo hay que entregarlo el viernes antes de las cuatro de la tarde.
(Spanish implies that four o'clock exactly will be too late.)

As the meaning of 'by' in English sentences of this kind is rather vague, you will have to decide whether in a particular context it means that the time itself is too late or not.

Ring the most appropriate choice of the three and cross out any that are wrong.

17 **Estoy de vuelta / para / antes de / a / las siete.**
I'll be back by seven.

18 **Te doy un telefonazo en cuanto sepa algo y / para el / en / antes del / viernes a lo más tarde.**
I'll give you a ring as soon as I have some news and by Friday at the latest.

19 **¿ / Para / Antes de / De / cuándo puedes hacerlo?**
By when can you do it?

VI Set expressions of time

ocho días, una semana a week

quince días, una quincena a fortnight

de hoy en ocho/quince días a week/fortnight today

el lunes que viene no, el otro a week on Monday

de aquí un año a year from now

los años veinte, treinta, etc. the twenties, thirties, etc.

dentro de una semana, tres días, dos meses, etc. in a week's, three days', two months' time (Note how confusing this is since one would expect it to mean 'within a week', etc. and it does not!)

en menos de una semana, etc. within a week, etc.

el siglo century

secular centuries-old, ancient (also 'secular' in some contexts)

finisecular fin-de-siècle (adj., as in el arte finisecular fin-de-siècle art)

When you have memorized any of the above that you did not already know, test yourself by translating:

> **20** this ancient stonework: **estas piedras** _ _ _ _ _ _ _ _ _
>
> **21** Thursday week: _ _   _ _ _ _ _ _   _ _ _   _ _ _ _ _   _ _ ,
> _ _   _ _ _ _
>
> **22** within three weeks: _ _   _ _ _ _ _   _ _ **tres semanas**
>
> **23** a fortnight: _ _ _ _ _ _   _ _ _ _ or _ _ _   _ _ _ _ _ _ _ _
>
> **24** the fifties: _ _ _   _ _ _ _   _ _ _ _ _ _ _ _ _
>
> **25** a month from now: _ _   _ _ _ _   _ _   _ _ _
>
> **26** a week: _ _ _ _   _ _ _ _ or _ _ _   _ _ _ _ _ _
>
> **27** in a year's time: _ _ _ _ _ _   _ _   _ _   _ _ _
>
> **28** a week today: _ _   _ _ _   _ _   _ _ _ _   _ _ _ _
>
> **29** fin-de-siècle malaise: **un malestar** _ _ _ _ _ _ _ _ _ _ _
>
> **30** This church was built five centuries ago.
> **Se construyó esta iglesia hace cinco** _ _ _ _ _ _.

Rhetorical signposts, like other kinds, are designed to prevent you getting lost. But instead of helping you when you are exploring geographically, they point you in the right direction and guide you through a written text. Many students find them difficult in English; perhaps that is why they do not even attempt to include them in their Spanish. This is a pity, since they help to guide the writer just as much as the reader. If you can manage to integrate them into your Spanish, you will instantly ratchet up its standard, making it more persuasive, sophisticated, and interesting to read.

Because of the widespread difficulties in English, the alphabetical list below will give not only a translation, but also an indication in parentheses of what each one implies.

a diferencia de unlike, in contrast to (to contrast two opposing elements)

además moreover, furthermore (to add a point that strengthens the previous one)

asimismo likewise, in the same way (to show that two points are in the same category)

cabe pensar/suponer que . . . There are grounds for thinking/ assuming s.th. (to show that the point about to be made is not proven but is grounded in logical supposition)

como cabía esperar as was (logically) to be expected (to show that the point was foreseeable)

de ahí que + subj. hence, that is why (to show that the next point follows logically from the one before)

You already know, but don't forget about:
dicho sea de paso incidentally (to alert the reader to the fact that the point being introduced does not advance the argument but is an interesting aside)

en cambio conversely, on the other hand (used to contrast two points)

en efecto, efectivamente indeed, sure enough (follows logically from and confirms previous point) NB a false friend: it does NOT mean 'in effect'.

en general, en términos generales on the whole, broadly speaking (acknowledges that following point will be somewhat schematic, simplified)

en resumen to sum up, briefly (indicates that material is now going to be pulled together and summarized)

evidentemente obviously (to introduce a point that is considered to be beyond argument by the writer/speaker)

menos mal que . . . it is just as well that . . . (to introduce a positive point that can be identified in an otherwise negative picture)

no obstante nevertheless, however, notwithstanding, in spite of (as well as being an alternative to **sin embargo**, this can precede a noun; it indicates that it will run counter to the previous point)

para colmo to crown it all (indicates exasperation/ indignation on part of speaker/writer and highlights most powerful point)

por consiguiente consequently (to indicate that the next point is the consequence of the one before)

por lo tanto therefore (to introduce a point which follows logically from the one before)

por otra parte besides, in addition (introduces new line of argument but one which complements previous one rather than running counter to it, in which case **en cambio** would be better)

por suerte/desgracia fortunately/ unfortunately (to show the writer's positive/negative attitude to what follows)

por un lado . . . por otro (lado) on the one hand . . . on the other (hand) (to balance two points against one another)

sin embargo however (to introduce a point that runs counter to the one before)

tanto x como y x just as much as y / x as well as y (to link two points and give them equal status)

Fit the signposts above into the gaps.

1 – 2 Me gusta viajar _ _ _ _ _ _ _ _ _ _ los problemas inevitables con equipaje, retrasos, hoteles sin construir, etcétera. _ _ _ _ _ _ _ _ me alegrara mucho cuando nos decidimos pasar el verano en Argentina.

I like travelling in spite of the inevitable problems with luggage, delays, unbuilt hotels, etc. That is why I was delighted when we decided to spend the summer in Argentina.

3 – 4 Era medianoche cuando llegamos por fin, cansados y exasperados por el retraso. _ _ _ _ _ _ _ _ _ _ , nos armamos de valor y en vez de acostarnos en seguida, salimos a explorar la ciudad. _ _ _ _ _ _ _ _ _ _ que no era muy buena idea, sobre todo a posteriori, pero nos dijimos 'Un día es un día'.

It was midnight when we finally arrived, tired and exasperated by the delay. However, we steeled ourselves and instead of going straight to bed, we went out to explore the city. It wasn't a very good idea, one might think, especially with the benefit of hindsight, but we said, 'What the heck'.

5 Nos enamoramos de la ciudad desde aquella primera noche. ¿Por qué? Por todo, pero _ _ _ _ _ _ _ _ _ _ _ _ _ _ _ _ _ _ _ _ , por su ambiente alegre y animado.

We fell in love with the city right from that first night. Why? Because of everything, but in a nutshell, because of its lively, animated atmosphere.

6 Tomamos muchas copas, cada una en un bar diferente. Al día siguiente, _ _ _   _ _   _ _ _ _ _ , no nos sentíamos muy bien.
We drank a lot, going from bar to bar. The next day, therefore, we were not feeling very well.

7 A mí me dolían la cabeza – por las copas –, la espalda – por el equipaje – y, _ _ _ _   _ _ _ _ _   los mosquitos me habían comido viva durante la noche.
For my part, I had a headache – from the drinking –, a backache – from the luggage – and, to crown it all, the mosquitos had eaten me alive during the night.

8 – **9** _ _ _   _ _ _ _   _ _ _ _ _   la maleta de mi novio se había extraviado; _ _ _ _ _   _ _ _   que le cabían una camiseta y unos tejanos míos.
The other thing was that my boyfriend's suitcase had gone astray; it was just as well that a tee-shirt and some jeans of mine fitted him.

10 – **11** _ _ _   _ _ _ _ _ _ _ _ _ _ _ _ _ , no había más remedio que pasar el día en el hotel hablando por teléfono con el aeropuerto.
_ _ _ _ _ _ _ _ _ _ _ _ _ _ , nuestro primer día en Buenos Aires no era exactamente divertido.
Consequently, we had no choice but to spend the day on the phone to the airport. Obviously, our first day in Buenos Aires was not exactly fun.

12 Pero nos dijeron que nos localizarían la maleta extraviada en menos de veinticuatro horas y, _ _   _ _ _ _ _ _ _ , a eso de las ocho de la tarde nos la entregaron en el hotel.
But they told us they would locate the missing suitcase within twenty-four hours and, sure enough, at about eight o'clock in the evening, it was delivered to the hotel.

13 – **14** Pasado aquel primer día difícil, empezamos a divertirnos de nuevo. Exploramos no solamente la ciudad sino el campo argentino también.
_ _ _   _ _   _ _ _ _   la gente nos trató muy bien y _ _ _ _ _ _ _ _   nos encantó el paisaje. _ _   _ _ _ _ _ _ _   los demás turistas que conocimos eran bastante menos simpáticos.
After that difficult first day, we started to enjoy ourselves again. We not only explored the city but the Argentinian countryside as well. On the one hand the people treated us very well and, on the other, we loved the scenery. The other tourists we met, however, were rather less pleasant.

15 – **16** _ _ _ _ _ _ , no habíamos ido a Argentina para estar con otros ingleses y norteamericanos y _   _ _ _ _ _ _ _ _ _ _ _   _ _ ellos, no queríamos pasar nuestro tiempo quejándonos de todo.
Furthermore, we had not gone to Argentina to be with other English people and Americans and, unlike them, we didn't want to spend our time complaining about everything.

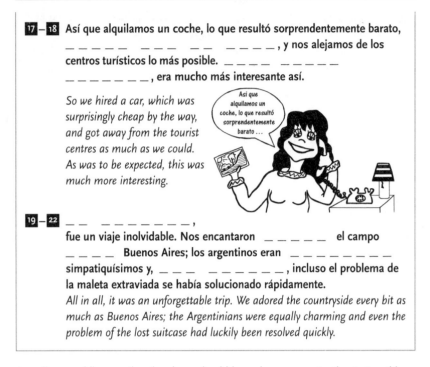

17 – 18 Así que alquilamos un coche, lo que resultó sorprendentemente barato, _ _ _ _ _ _ _ _ _ _ _ _ _ _ , y nos alejamos de los centros turísticos lo más posible. _ _ _ _ _ _ _ _ _ _ _ _ _ _ _ , era mucho más interesante así.

So we hired a car, which was surprisingly cheap by the way, and got away from the tourist centres as much as we could. As was to be expected, this was much more interesting.

19 – 22 _ _ _ _ _ _ _ _ _ _ , fue un viaje inolvidable. Nos encantaron _ _ _ _ _ el campo _ _ _ _ Buenos Aires; los argentinos eran _ _ _ _ _ _ _ _ simpatiquísimos y, _ _ _ _ _ _ _ _ _ , incluso el problema de la maleta extraviada se había solucionado rápidamente.

All in all, it was an unforgettable trip. We adored the countryside every bit as much as Buenos Aires; the Argentinians were equally charming and even the problem of the lost suitcase had luckily been resolved quickly.

As well as providing practice, the above should have drawn your attention to two things: first, that signposts are just as useful in a narrative as in an argument and, second, that you need to be flexible in how you translate them, since the context may well demand a choice other than the ones given in the list.

Here is a selection of ten abstract constructions that will upgrade the quality of your written Spanish:

cada vez más/menos more and more / less and less
al fin y al cabo when all's said and done, at the end of the day
para bien o para mal for good or ill
una vez por todas once and for all
tarde o temprano sooner or later
un cuento de nunca acabar a never-ending story (used for something that you would rather would come to an end)
con razón (o sin ella) rightly (or wrongly)
sin ambages without beating about the bush
hoy en día nowadays
ir de mal en peor to go from bad to worse (note that **en**)

Make sure you know these by heart and when you are writing in Spanish, keep asking yourself where you are going. Try to track your own argument by using as many rhetorical signposts as you can.

Test yourself by trying to write out all ten of the above phrases from memory: cover up the English in the list below and see how many you can produce spontaneously. When you have done as many as you can, uncover the English and draw lines to match the ones you have written down to their meanings. Then use the remaining meanings to help you remember the ones you could not produce purely from memory.

---

23 – 30

for good or ill ....

nowadays ....

at the end of the day ....

rightly or wrongly ....

more and more/less and less ....

without beating about the bush ....

sooner or later ....

to go from bad to worse ....

a never-ending story ....

once and for all ....

The scoring is like this:

▶ if you manage to write all ten down unprompted, you score 8 points.

▶ if you got 7 or more right unprompted and the others you also got once you looked at the English: 7 points.

▶ if you got fewer than 7 unprompted, but got everything once you looked at the English: 6 points.

From those 8, 7, or 6 points, deduct 1 point for any gap or mistake (including an accent!).

Upgrade your vocabulary: History

Do you find you hesitate or slow down when you need to use numbers in Spanish (in dates as well as in other contexts)? Do you make mistakes when you need to write dates or read them aloud? Today's first exercise is designed to increase your confidence and accuracy with dates.

KNOW YOUR DATES!

Do the following exercise orally first and time yourself with a stopwatch. Say aloud in Spanish:

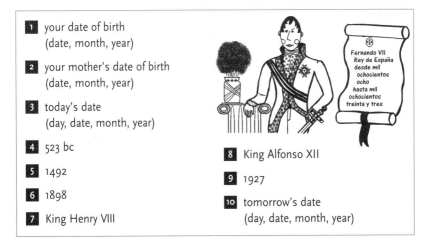

Fernando VII
Rey de España
desde mil
ochocientos
ocho
hasta mil
ochocientos
treinta y tres

1 your date of birth
(date, month, year)

2 your mother's date of birth
(date, month, year)

3 today's date
(day, date, month, year)

4 523 bc

5 1492

6 1898

7 King Henry VIII

8 King Alfonso XII

9 1927

10 tomorrow's date
(day, date, month, year)

Speed and confidence

Under one minute is good. Between one and two minutes is not bad. More than two minutes suggests you need more practice. Try repeatedly opening a big dictionary at random and reading the page number in Spanish as fast as you can. Close your eyes and press a few keys on a calculator; then open your eyes and read out the number displayed as fast as you can. Go on until you are satisfied that your speed in Spanish is close to English.

Accuracy

Check on this by writing out in words the answers you gave for the exercise above. Score 1 point for each completely correct answer.

1 ....

2 ....

3 ....

4 ....

5 ....

6 ....

7 ....

8 ....

9 ....

10 ....

HISTORICAL VOCABULARY

Historical vocabulary overlaps with political vocabulary. Where it does, you have had some practice on Day 5. The remainder of today's work covers other word-groups that you could find useful when dealing with historical subjects.

The exercise below is designed to give you practice in dredging your memory and turning passive knowledge into active knowledge. You have probably come across all the words in the exercise, but may not have used many of them yourself.

In the first instance, see how many of the gaps you can fill in without looking up the answers. Score one point if you can fill in all the gaps in a group and a half point if you fill in some gaps correctly. When you have done your best from your existing knowledge and calculated your score, fill in the remaining gaps by consulting the answer section.

11 From **la guerra** *war*

el guerr _ _ _   *warrior*

la guerr _ _ _ _   *guerrilla war(fare)*

el/la guerr _ _ _ _ _ _ _ / **-a**   *guerrilla fighter*

12 From **el imperio** *empire*

_ **mper** _ _ _   *imperial*   _ **mper** _ _ _ _   *imperious*

_ **mper** _ _   *to rule, prevail*   **el** _ **mper** _ _ _ _   *emperor*

_ **mper** _ _ _ _   *prevailing (adj.)*   **la** _ **mper** _ _ _ _ _   *empress*

13 From **la edad** *age*

la _ _ _ _ **de** _ _ _   *the Golden Age* (Classical mythology or figurative; not the Spanish Renaissance **el Siglo de Oro**)

la _ _ _ _ **de** _ _ _ _ _ _   *Bronze Age*

la _ _ _ _ **de** _ _ _ _ _ _   *Stone Age*

la _ _ _ _   _ _ _ _ _   *Middle Ages*

14 From **la victoria** *victory*
vict _ _ _ _ _ _   *victorious*
_ _ **vict** _   *undefeated, unbeaten*

15 From **vencer** (some spelling changes needed – see Day 24) *to defeat*
_ _ **venc** _ _ _ _   *invincible, unbeatable*
el/la venc _ _ _ _ /- _ _ _   *the winner, victor*

16 From **el rey** *the king*

el _ _ _ **rey** *viceroy*	**el re** _ _ _ *kingdom*
la re _ _ _ *queen*	**re** _ _ _ _ *to reign*

17 From **el yugo** *yoke*
_ _ _ **yug** _ _   *to subjugate*

18 From **la frontera** *border, frontier* – adj. for 'border' (as in 'border controls or disputes')
controles o disputas fronter _ _ _ _

19 From **la corte** *court* – (not to be confused with **el corte** – the cut of a garment, as in the famous Spanish shop called **El Corte Inglés**)
cort _ _   *courteous, polite* (note that this is an exception to the basic agreement rules since the feminine is the same as the masculine)
el cort _ _ _ _ _   *courtier*   **la cort** _ _ _ _ _   *courtesan*
And you remember the Spanish Parliament from Day 5:
_ _ _   _ _ _ _ _ _

20 From **rico** and **pobre** and **noble**
la ri _ _ _ _ _   *wealth*
la pobr _ _ _   *poverty*
la nobl _ _ _   *nobility*

21 From **antiguo** *old, antique, ancient*
la antig _ _ _ _ _   *antiquity, antique* (as for piece of furniture), and also
NB *seniority*
(think about the spelling here: how do you indicate that the **u** needs to be heard and it is not just there to harden the **g** as in **guerra**? There will be more on this on Day 24)

22 From **servir** *to serve* (radical-changing as **pedir** – see Day 15)
el s _ **rv** _ _ _ _ _ , **la s** _ **rv** _ _ _ _ _   *servant*
s _ **rv** _ _ _ _ _   *helpful*
s _ **rv** _ l   *servile*

23 From **el/la esclavo/-a** *slave*
la esclav _ _ _ _   *slavery, bondage*

24 From **el héroe** *hero*
la hero _ _ _ *heroine, heroin* (think about the stress rules for this one)
el hero _ _ _ _ *heroism* (. . . and this one)
hero _ _ _ *heroic*

25 From **la revolución** *revolution*
el/la revoluc _ _ _ _ _ _ _ /-a *revolutionary*
_ _ _ _ _ _ rrevoluc _ _ _ _ _ _ _ *counter-revolutionary*

26 From **la lucha** *struggle, wrestling*
luch _ _ con *to struggle*
la _ _ _ _ _ de las _ _ _ _ _ _ *class struggle*

27 From **la rebelión** *rebellion*
rebel _ _ _ _ _ _ _ _ _ _ *to rebel against*
el/la rebel _ _ *rebel*

28 From **la tregua** *truce*
_ _ _ tregua *relentless(ly)*

29 From **la paz** *peace*
_ pa _ _ _ _ _ _ *to pacify, soothe* (some spelling changes needed – see Day 24)
_ pa _ _ _ _ _ *peaceable, calm*
pa _ _ _ _ _ _ *pacific*

30 From **la historia** *history, story*
hist _ _ _ _ _ *historic, historical*
el/la hist _ _ _ _ _ _ _ _ /- _ _ _ *historian*

A radical overhaul of radical-changing verbs

To be right every time when you use radical-changing verbs, you need to know three things:
- *first, whether the verb you are using is radical-changing at all;*
- *second, if it is, which of the three patterns it belongs to;*
- *third, how to conjugate that particular pattern.*

Contrary to what most students think, the first two of these points are the most problematic. The third demands one initial effort and is straightforward ever after. The exercises today give some attention to all three areas but emphasis is put on the third one because it is the easiest to remedy on one's own, and getting it right can make an immediate and tangible difference to accuracy.

I How do you know if a verb is radical-changing?

Unfortunately, there is no completely reliable rule to follow. Sometimes it is possible to make an educated guess based on cognate items. For example, if you didn't know whether **enterrar** [to bury] was radical-changing or not, you could guess that it was from the noun, **la tierra**. So if you are faced with having to make a guess, think about any cognate words you know; it will not work every time, but it will sometimes be helpful.

In the following exercise, find a cognate and, based on that, decide if the verb given is likely to be radical-changing or not by ringing the correct answer.

		Radical-changing?
1 **rodar** *to roll* la **rueda** *wheel*		~~Yes~~ / No
2 **remar** *to row* (as in a rowing boat) el **remo** *oar*		Yes / ~~No~~
3 **contar** *to (re)count* la **cuenta** *short story*		~~Yes~~ No

II How do you know which pattern a radical-changing verb belongs to?

i) All **-ar** and **-er** radical-changing verbs belong to the same pattern, referred to as the 'first pattern' in this book.

ii) The radical-changing **-ir** verbs can belong to either the second or the third pattern. There is no hard and fast way of telling which, alas. However, once you have learnt a reasonable number of verbs, things start to get easier, since it is possible to match an unfamiliar verb to one you already know belongs to a particular pattern. For example, if you know **sentir** [to feel] (second pattern) and **pedir** [to ask for] (third pattern), it is easy to guess derivatives like **presentir** [to have a presentiment] (second pattern) and **impedir** [to prevent] (third pattern).

iii) Not only that, but if you know **divertir** [to entertain] (second) and **reñir** [to scold] (third), it is reasonable to guess that **invertir** [to invest] and **teñir** [to dye] will belong to the second and third pattern respectively (and they do). Therefore, the more scrupulously you learn as you go along and the more observantly you read, the easier it will gradually become.

III **How do you know when to make the radical changes?**
The basic rule for radical-changing verbs is that the changes occur when the stress falls on the stem of the verb (the part that is not the ending).

i) The first pattern – the one to which all **-ar** and **-er** radical-changing verbs belong – follows this rule completely. For example:

   entender   [to understand] (stress on ending, so no radical change)
   entiendo   [I understand] (stress on stem, so change occurs)

   Note that this is another reason for stressing verb-forms correctly even in one's head.

ii) In the second pattern, there is a two-letter change that conforms to this rule, but an anomalous one-letter change in certain other places. These simply have to be learnt. For example:

   mentir   [to lie]
   miento   [I lie] (etc., follows the first pattern)

Here are the anomalous one-letter changes. They are anomalous because the stress is on the ending of the verb and not on the stem as the basic rule dictates:

   mintamos, mintáis   (first- and second-persons plural of the present subjunctive)
   mintiendo   (gerund/present participle)
   mintió   (third-person singular of the preterite)
   mintieron   (third-person plural of the preterite)

Because the imperfect subjunctive is formed from the third-person plural of the preterite and, as you see, there is an anomalous one-letter change here, it will be found all the way through the imperfect subjunctive of these verbs:

   mintiera   mintiéramos
   mintieras   mintierais
   mintiera   mintieran

iii) The third pattern only has a one-letter change, which it makes in all the same places as the second pattern, namely, where the stress falls on the stem, as one would expect, and also in the same anomalous cases. For example:

pedir [to ask for]
pido [I ask for] (etc.)

Anomalies occur in the same places as the second pattern:

pidamos, pidáis (first- and second-person plural of present subjunctive)
pidiendo (gerund/present participle)
pidió (third-person singular of preterite)
pidieron (third-person plural of preterite)

The imperfect subjunctive also has the anomalous change throughout, just like the second pattern:

pidiera, pidieras, etc.

Build up your confidence and speed by filling in the following table. All the verbs in it are radical-changing. You will know which are first pattern because they are all the **-ar** and **-er** ones. For the **-ir** verbs, [2] or [3] after the infinitive will tell you whether they are second or third pattern.

> **4** (yo) **medir** [3] *to measure* (preterite): _ _ _ _
>
> **5** (tú) **divertirse** [2] *to enjoy oneself* (present): _ _ _ _ _ _ _ _ _ _ _
>
> **6** (él) **entender** *to understand* (imp. subj.): _ _ _ _ _ _ _ _ _ _ _
>
> **7** (ella) **soltar** *to free* (future): _ _ _ _ _ _ _
>
> **8** (nosotros) **referir** [2] *to refer* (imp. subj.): _ _ _ _ _ _ _ _ _ _ _ _ _
>
> **9** (vosotros) **pedir** [3] *to ask for* (present subjunctive): _ _ _ _ _ _
>
> **10** (ellos) **soler** *to be wont to* (imperfect): _ _ _ _ _ _ _

If you did not recognize any of these verbs or if you knew them but did not know that they were radical-changing or, lastly, if you knew them to be radical-changing but did not know which pattern they were, make sure you have copied them into your own notes and memorized them.

The next set will be a mixture of regular radical-changing and non-radical-changing verbs. The pattern for the **-ir** radical-changers will not be given either this time. Test your existing level of knowledge by filling in as many of the answers as you can without looking up and score your result accordingly. Then refer to the answer section to correct any errors and make good any gaps, again remembering to transfer into your own notes and learn by heart what you did not already know.

11 (yo) **serrar** *to saw*   present subjunctive: _ _ _ _ _ _

12 (tú) **errar** *to roam*   present: _ _ _ _ _

13 (él) **herrar** *to shoe horse*   future: _ _ _ _ _ _ _

14 (ella) **cerrar** *to close*   imperfect: _ _ _ _ _ _ _

15 (Vd.) **herir** *to wound*   imperfect subjunctive: _ _ _ _ _ _ _

16 (nosotros) **cubrir** *to cover*   preterite: _ _ _ _ _ _ _ _

17 (vosotros) **sentir** *to feel*   present subjunctive: _ _ _ _ _ _ _

18 (ellos) **reñir** *to scold*   present: _ _ _ _ _

19 (ellas) **vestir** *to dress*   gerund/present participle: _ _ _ _ _ _ _ _ _

20 (Vds.) **pudrir** *to rot*   preterite: _ _ _ _ _ _ _ _ _

For the last exercise today:

▶ first, fill in the English translations for the alphabetical list of radical-changing verbs below;

▶ secondly, put 2 or 3 in the empty brackets after the **-ir** ones according to which pattern you think they follow;

▶ finally, choose one to fill each gap in the sentences below. You will have to decide which tense and mood to use as well. Each verb from the list will be used once.

colgar   ....
conferir [   ] ....
defender   ....
doler   ....
embestir [   ] ....
impedir [   ]   ....
invertir [   ] ....
moverse   ....
presentir [   ] ....
resolver   ....

21 Ustedes me están _ _ _ _ _ _ _ _ _ _ _ _ un gran honor invitándome a su cena anual.
You do me a great honour inviting me to your annual dinner.

22 El perro se _ _ _ _ _ _ la cola al ver llegar a su amo.
The dog wagged his tail when he saw his master coming.

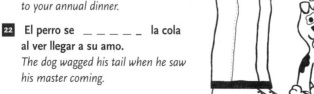

23 El tonto _ _ _ _ _ _ _ _ todo su dinero en ello; ya le había dicho yo
que lo perdería y en efecto así pasó.
The fool invested all his money in it; I'd told him he'd lose it and that's exactly
what happened.

24 El muy grosero me _ _ _ _ _ el teléfono.
That rude man actually hung up on me.

25 ¡Cuánto me _ _ _ _ _ la cabeza!
My head really aches!

26 Todos mis problemas de dinero se _ _ _ _ _ _ _ _ _ _ _ _ si me
tocara la lotería.
All my money problems would be resolved if I won the lottery.

27 El toro _ _ _ _ _ _ _ _ _ contra nosotros.
The bull charged at us.

28 Cuando va a haber tormenta, suelo presentirlo, pero aquella vez no sentí
nada y, en cambio, fue mi marido quien lo _ _ _ _ _ _ _ _ _ .
When there is going to be a storm, I usually feel it in advance, but that time I
didn't at all and it was in fact my husband who had the presentiment.

29 Sé que es un tipo bastante agresivo, pero ¿por qué no te
 _ _ _ _ _ _ _ _ _ nunca?
I know he's quite an aggressive type, but why don't you ever defend yourself?

30 Decía que quería hacerlo pero en realidad quería que nosotros le
 _ _ _ _ _ _ _ _ _ _ _ _ _ seguir adelante.
He used to say he wanted to do it but in fact he wanted us to prevent him from
going ahead.

Musical vocabulary is not only worth knowing in its own right, but is to be found in a very wide range of other contexts too, because of the figurative and metaphorical importance of this lexical domain. You only have to think of words like 'harmony' and 'orchestrate', to realize that this is the case in English; in Spanish, it is just as true (although not always directly equivalent to English usage).

el concierto concert, concerto, recital
   (BUT also agreement, harmony)
concertar to tune (up), be in tune (BUT
   also, to arrange, agree)

la concertación harmonization,
   agreement
desconcertar to disconcert
desconcertante disconcerting

Ring the right answer:

> **1** Based on **concierto**, guess whether **concertar**
>   and **desconcertar** are radical-changing: Yes / No

el acorde chord
acorde in tune (both literally and
   figuratively)
desacorde discordant, out of tune,
   conflicting
acordar to agree (on)
el acuerdo agreement (. . . so will
   acordar be radical-changing?)
el acordeón accordion

el compás tempo, (musical) beat
   (NB – false friend: NOT a compass)
acompasado rhythmic, regular (of beat)
desacompasado out of step/time,
   irregular

la armonía harmony
armonizar to harmonize

> **2** Guess *harmonica:* _ _ _ _ _ _ _ _ _ _
>
> **3** Guess *harmonious:* _ _ _ _ _ _ _ _ _ _
>
> **4** Guess *harmonization:* _ _ _ _ _ _ _ _ _ _ _ _ _ _

la canción song
la canción de cuna lullaby
(la cuna cradle)

el cancionero collection of early
Spanish poetry
cantarín/-ina singsong
el pájaro cantor songbird

la tiple soprano
atiplado high-pitched

afinar to tune (instrument or motor)
(BUT ALSO to perfect)

---

5 Guess *a piano tuner:* un/una _ _ _ _ _ _ _ _ _ /- _ _ _ _ de pianos

---

desafinarse to go out of tune
desafinado out of tune

la orquesta orchestra
orquestar to orchestrate
(literally and figuratively)
orquestal orchestral

dirigir to conduct (an orchestra), to
direct, to address
el/la director/-ora de orquesta
conductor (music)

grabar to record (audio or video)
la grabación recording

WORDSEARCH

Find one word from each of the above groups written horizontally or vertically in the grid. Then copy it in the space provided below and see how many of the cognates (and their meanings) you can reproduce from memory. Score one point for reproducing all of a group and a half mark for getting some but not all.

L	A	U	R	M	V	Y	N	N	D	E	N
D	I	E	L	A	C	O	R	D	E	J	U
L	O	L	G	I	A	L	E	R	S	D	E
E	N	C	L	I	N	J	G	L	C	E	L
O	E	O	E	Z	T	R	R	H	O	S	A
C	D	M	E	B	A	X	A	B	N	A	R
E	O	P	V	A	R	O	B	C	C	F	E
P	Y	Á	S	P	Í	J	A	L	E	I	A
Q	U	S	D	A	N	C	R	U	R	N	D
O	R	Q	U	E	S	T	A	L	T	A	I
O	N	B	U	A	T	I	P	L	A	D	O
R	T	O	B	J	H	N	S	D	N	O	M
L	A	A	R	M	O	N	Í	A	T	R	I
A	D	I	R	I	G	I	R	E	E	O	R

---

6 _ _ _ _ _ _ _ _ _ _ _ _ _ _ _ _ *disconcerting*

_ _   _ _ _ _ _ _ _ _ ....

_ _ _ _ _ _ _ _ ....

_ _   _ _ _ _ _ _ _ _ _ _ ....

_ _ _ _ _ _ _ _ _ _ ....

7 _ _   _ _ _ _ _ _   *chord*

_ _ _ _ _   ....

_ _ _ _ _ _ _   ....

_ _ _ _ _ _   ....

_ _   _ _ _ _ _ _   ....

_ _   _ _ _ _ _ _ _   ....

8 _ _   _ _ _ _ _ _   *tempo*

_ _ _ _ _ _ _ _   ....

_ _ _ _ _ _ _ _ _ _   ....

9 _ _   _ _ _ _ _ _ _   *harmony*

_ _ _ _ _ _ _ _   ....

_ _   _ _ _ _ _ _ _   ....

_ _ _ _ _ _ _ _   ....

_ _   _ _ _ _ _ _ _ _ _ _   ....

10 _ _ _ _ _ _ _ _   *singsong*

_ _   _ _ _ _ _ _   ....

_ _   _ _ _ _ _ _   _ _   _ _ _ _   ....

_ _   _ _ _ _ _ _ _ _   ....

_ _   _ _ _ _ _   _ _ _ _ _   ....

11 _ _ _ _ _ _ _ _   *high-pitched*

_ _   _ _ _ _ _   ....

12 _ _ _ _ _ _ _ _ _ _   *out of tune*

_ _ _ _ _   ....

_ _   _ _ _ _ _ _ _   _ _   _ _ _ _ _   ....

_ _ _ _ _ _ _ _ _   ....

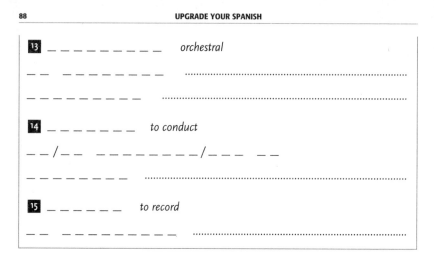

13 _ _ _ _ _ _ _ _ _   *orchestral*

_ _ _ _ _ _ _ _ _ ....

_ _ _ _ _ _ _ _ _ ....

14 _ _ _ _ _ _ _   *to conduct*

_ _ / _ _ _ _ _ _ _ _ _ _ / _ _ _ _ _

_ _ _ _ _ _ _ ....

15 _ _ _ _ _ _   *to record*

_ _ _ _ _ _ _ _ _ _ ....

Now here are some musical instruments and some musicians who play them, followed by a few more items connected to popular music:

la guitarra guitar (notice, and remember to pronounce, the double 'r')

16 *guitarist:* **el/la** _ _ _ _ _ _ _ _ _ _ _

el tambor drum	**la batería** drums, drum kit	**la viola** viola
la pandereta tambourine	(BUT also car and	**el/la viola** viola player
el/la batería drummer	artillery battery)	**el violín** violin

17 *violinist:* **el/la** _ _ _ _ _ _ _ _ _ _

el violón double bass	**el/la violoncelista, chelista** 'cellist
el/la violón double bass player	
el violoncelo, el chelo 'cello	**la trompeta** trumpet

18 *trumpeter:* **el/la** _ _ _ _ _ _ _ _ _ _ _

la trompa elephant's trunk	**el clarín** bugle
la trompa de caza hunting horn	**el clarinete** clarinet

19 *clarinettist:* **el/la** _ _ _ _ _ _ _ _ _ _ _ _

la flauta flute

20 *flautist:* el/la _ _ _ _ _ _ _ _ _

aflautado high-pitched, flutey
el flautín piccolo
la flauta dulce recorder

un éxito a hit, as well as a success (NB is a false friend: not an exit!)
la lista de éxitos hit parade
tener éxito to be a success

la letra lyrics (of song – singular in Spanish), letter (of alphabet), handwriting
el/la letrista lyricist
el letrero sign
letrado learned
iletrado illiterate

el/la compositor/-ora composer
la composición composition (musical or pictorial, but not schoolchildren's word for an essay!)
componer to compose
descompuesto upset, indisposed

The following words need no translation – you don't have to learn them!
los blues
el jazz
el reggae
el rocanrol
el walkman

21 Guess *a compact disc:* _ _ _ _ _ _ _ _ _ _ _ _ _ _ _

When you think you know the vocabulary listed above, spot-check by filling the gaps in the sentences below. If you find it very difficult, or make a lot of mistakes, the chances are you need to go back over all the vocabulary from today, not just the selection of items that crop up below.

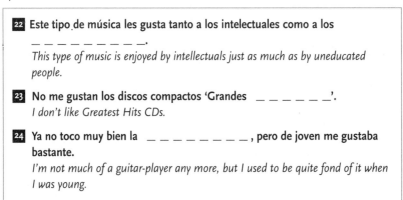

22 Este tipo de música les gusta tanto a los intelectuales como a los

_ _ _ _ _ _ _ _ _.
This type of music is enjoyed by intellectuals just as much as by uneducated people.

23 No me gustan los discos compactos 'Grandes _ _ _ _ _ _'.
I don't like Greatest Hits CDs.

24 Ya no toco muy bien la _ _ _ _ _ _ _ _ _, pero de joven me gustaba bastante.
I'm not much of a guitar-player any more, but I used to be quite fond of it when I was young.

25   Me cuesta comprender _ _   _ _ _ _ _ de muchas canciones populares, pero mi nieta me la explica.
I have trouble understanding the lyrics of a lot of pop songs, but my granddaughter explains them to me.

26   El nuevo _ _ _ _ _ _ _ del grupo es estupendo; ¿lo has oído tocar?
The new drummer in the group is brilliant; have you heard him?

27   Cuando Machado habló en un poema célebre de la 'España de _ _ _ _ _ _ _ _ _ ', se refería a la España tradicional.
When in a famous poem, Machado wrote of the 'Spain of the tambourine', he meant traditional Spain.

28   A Elvis Presley se le conoce como el rey del _ _ _ _ _ _ _ _ _.
Elvis Presley is known as the king of rock'n'roll.

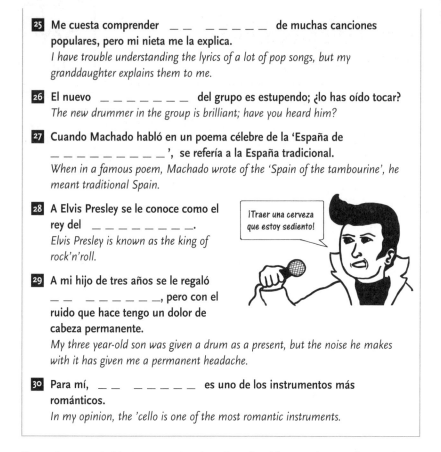

¡Traer una cerveza que estoy sediento!

29   A mi hijo de tres años se le regaló _ _   _ _ _ _ _ _, pero con el ruido que hace tengo un dolor de cabeza permanente.
My three year-old son was given a drum as a present, but the noise he makes with it has given me a permanent headache.

30   Para mí, _ _   _ _ _ _ _ es uno de los instrumentos más románticos.
In my opinion, the 'cello is one of the most romantic instruments.

If you play a musical instrument other than those listed here, or have an interest in any specialized type of music not included in today's vocabulary, be sure to look up all you need to be able to talk or write about it if the opportunity arises.

Verbs with prepositions: Nasty but learnable

The use of prepositions in Spanish only sometimes matches their usage in English. If you listen to Spaniards speaking English, you may notice that even quite competent linguists make mistakes with 'in', 'on', and 'at', for example.

VERBS WITH DEPENDENT PREPOSITIONS

The exercises today tackle just one corner of this area: Spanish verbs with dependent prepositions that do not match English usage. The idea is to achieve accuracy for a realistic number of constructions so that you can make a point of using at least some of them, thereby upgrading your written and spoken Spanish.

A second objective is to heighten your awareness so that you can build on what you covered today in the future. The impact of dependent prepositions on the use of pronouns is also considered and practised at the end of the section.

The first step towards the building-on is always to note down any dependent preposition when you learn a new verb, so that the infinitive is linked from the outset with the right preposition in your memory. Good dictionaries include this information by giving examples, so make sure you read the whole entry and actively look for any prepositions that are found with a verb.

I   English and Spanish have different prepositions

consistir en to consist of	**hablar con** to speak to
depender de to depend on	**quejarse de** to complain about
enterarse de to find out about	

II   Spanish has a preposition where a likely English equivalent has none

acercarse a to approach, go over to, draw close to

acordarse de to remember

arrepentirse de (radical-changing, second pattern) to regret

confiar en, no fiarse de (both irreg., cf. **continuar**) to trust, not to trust

jugar a to play (a game or sport) – (think of **el juego** and you know it is radical-changing, don't you?)

llamar por teléfono/telefonear a to telephone

olvidarse de to forget (BUT this construction is often replaced by a reverse one without a preposition at all – think of **gustar**. For example: 'I forgot to send him/her a Christmas card.' – **Me olvidé de mandarle un**

Christmas (possible, but unlikely);
Se me olvidó mandarle un
Christmas (more common). Or: 'I'm
so sorry: I completely forgot' (cf. the

English expression 'it slipped my
mind') – **Cuánto lo siento: se me
olvidó por completo**
parecerse a (irreg.) to resemble

III   Spanish has no preposition where a likely English equivalent requires one

mirar to look at
buscar to look for (spelling changes
     needed – see Day 24)
esperar to wait/hope for

pedir to ask for
pagar to pay for (spelling changes
     needed – see Day 24)

Fill the gaps in the following sentences:

1   **Lo siento: _ _ me _ _ _ _ _ _ tu libro. Ya te lo devolveré mañana.**
I'm sorry: I forgot your book. I'll give it back tomorrow.

2   **¡Qué tacaño es! Después de todo lo que había hecho, ni siquiera me _ _ _ _ una taza de café.**
He's so stingy. After all I'd done, he didn't even buy me a cup of coffee.

3   **_ _ _ _ _ _ _ _ _ _ _ la mesa donde estaba sentado el flautista.**
I went over to the table where the flautist was sitting.

4   **La casa _ _ _ _ _ _ _ _ _ _ _ dos apartamentos separados.**
The house consists of two separate flats.

5   **Si _ _ mí _ _ _ _ _ _ _ _ _ _ _ _, diría que sí en seguida.**
If it were up to me, I'd say yes straight away. (Hint: translate 'if it depended on me')

6   **No _ _ _ _ _ _ _ _ _ _ _ mi abuela materna, que murió cuando yo tenía tres años.**
I don't remember my maternal grandmother, who died when I was three.

7   **_ _ _ _ _ _ mis padres una vez por semana.**
I ring my parents once a week.

8   **Te perdiste porque nunca _ _ _ _ _ los letreros.**
You got lost because you never look at the signs.

9   **Los chicos se habían ido al parque a _ _ _ _ _ _l fútbol.**
The boys had gone to the park to play football.

10 Si te _ _ _ _ dinero, no te fíes.
If he asks you for money, be on your guard. (Notice how **fiarse de** does not need the **de** when it has this stand-alone meaning of 'smelling a rat', 'being on one's guard'.)

11 Puedes _ _ _ _ _ _ _ _ _ _ mí; cuéntamelo todo, que no te traicionaré.
You can trust me; tell me the whole story and I won't give you away.

12 _ _ _ _ _ _ _ _ el tranvía desde hacía veinticinco minutos.
He had been waiting for the tram for twenty-five minutes.

13 _ _ _ _ _ _ _ _ _ _ _ _ _ _ su crueldad para con ella.
He lived to regret his cruelty towards her. (*Hint:* for 'lived to regret', just use the preterite of the verb 'to regret'.)

14 _ _ _ _ _ _ _ _ _I retraso, pero no sirvió para nada.
I complained about the delay, but it didn't do any good.

15 _ _ _ _ _ la cara de su hijo entre las riadas de gente saliendo de la estación.
She looked for her son's face amongst the crowds pouring out of the station.

16 Estaba _ _ _ _ _ _ _ _ _ _ _ _ _ el director de orquesta sobre el programa de conciertos planificado para el verano.
He was talking to the conductor about the planned summer concert programme.

17 _ _ _ _ _ _ _ _ _ _ _ ello por pura casualidad.
I found out about it completely by coincidence.

18 De pequeño era la viva imagen de mi padre, pero en estos días todo el mundo me dice que _ _ _ _ _ _ _ _ _ más _ mi madre.
When I was little I was the spitting image of my father but these days everyone says I look more like my mother.

19–**20** No _ _ _ _ _ _ de la memoria; apúntalo, que si no, _ _ _ _ _ _ _ _ _ _ _ _ .
Don't trust your memory; jot it down or else you'll forget. (*Hint:* remember to use the reverse construction for 'forget', like 'it will slip your mind'.)

IV A common confusion

Do not mistake the personal **a** for a dependent preposition. There is no visible or audible difference between the two uses of the word **a**, but you do need to know what you are dealing with, or else you will make mistakes with pronouns. For example:

Buscó a su madre. [He/she looked for his/her mother.]

This **a** is the personal **a**. It is there because **madre** is a specific human being and not because **buscar** demands it as a dependent preposition. How do we know? The test is to put a non-human object in the place of **madre** and then see if the **a** is required:

Buscó su cartera. [He/she looked for his/her satchel.]

There is no **a** here. That proves that the **a** was there for the **madre** and not because **buscar** needed it. Therefore, both **madre** and **cartera** are direct objects and if they were to be replaced with a pronoun, it would be the direct object pronoun that would be needed in both cases:

La buscó. [He/she looked for her/it.]

Contrast this with **telefonear a**. Here the **a** is a dependent preposition. The test is to see if it needs to be there for a non-human being. For example:

Telefoneó a la universidad. [He/she telephoned the university.]

Yes, it is there even though **universidad** is not human, so the **a** is there for the verb. Notice that when a verb like this, which demands **a** as a dependent preposition, has a human object, the **a** takes on a double function:

Telefoneó a su hija. [He/she telephoned his/her daughter.]

This **a** is both a dependent preposition and a personal **a**.

So when the object of a verb with a dependent **a** needs to be replaced by a pronoun, it cannot use the direct object. Where the direct object is a place, it is a safer to choose to use **allí**. Thus the university example 'Telefoneó a la universidad' would become 'Telefoneó allí'.

When the object is a person, an indirect object pronoun is needed. So the daughter example 'Telefoneó a su hija', would become 'Le telefoneó (a ella)'.

Practise distinguishing between these two uses of **a** in the following exercise.

i) **Vio a su mujer.** [He saw his wife.]

> *Step 1:* Test if this is a personal **a** or a dependent preposition demanded by the verb **ver** by replacing the human **mujer** with an inanimate object.

Ring the correct answer:

21 a) **Vio la guitarra.**   b) **Vio a la guitarra.**   [He saw the guitar.]

If you have ringed (a), that means you think the **a** is a personal **a** and that **mujer** and **guitarra** are both normal direct objects.
If you ringed (b), that means you think that **ver** demands the dependent preposition **a**, in which case **mujer** and **guitarra** are both indirect objects.

> *Step 2:* Replace **mujer** with the right pronoun.

Ring the right answer.

> **22** Which sentence means *He saw her?*
> a) **La vio** (direct object)   OR   b) **Le vio** (indirect object)

ii) **Se parece a su hermana.** [She looks like her sister.]

Follow Steps 1 and 2 as above and ring the right answers:

> **23** Which sentence means *She looks like a Greek statue?*
> a) **Se parece una estatua griega;**   OR   b) **Se parece a una estatua griega.**

> **24** Therefore to replace **hermana** with a pronoun – *She looks like her* – would it be correct to say:
> a) **Se la parece;**   OR   b) **Se le parece?**

iii) **En esta novela, el protagonista mata a su madre en el último capítulo.**
[In this novel, the protagonist kills his mother in the last chapter.]

Ring the correct answer:

> **25** Which sentence means *the protagonist kills a fly?*
> a) **El protagonista mata una mosca;**   OR
> b) **El protagonista mata a una mosca.**

> **26** Therefore to replace **madre** with a pronoun – *he kills her* – would it be correct to say:
> a) **El protagonista la mata en el último capítulo;**   OR
> b) **El protagonista le mata en el último capítulo?**

iv) **Ramón llama por teléfono a su novia todos los días.**
[Ramón phones his girlfriend every day.]

> **27** Which sentence means *Ramón phones the bank every day?*
> a) **Ramón llama el banco todos los días;**   OR
> b) **Ramón llama al banco todos los días.**

> **28** Therefore, to replace **novia** with a pronoun – *Ramón phones her* – would it be correct to say:
> a) **Ramón la llama todos los días;**   OR
> b) **Ramón le llama todos los días?**

(v) **Ramón besa a su novia todas las noches.**
[Ramón kisses his girlfriend every night.]

> **29** Which sentence means *Ramón kisses the Bible every night?*
> a) **Ramón besa la Biblia todas las noches;**
> OR
> b) **Ramón besa a la Biblia todas las noches.**

> **30** Therefore, to replace **novia** with a pronoun this time – *Ramón kisses her –* would it be correct to say:
> a) **Ramón la besa todas las noches;** OR
> b) **Ramón le besa todas las noches?**

Knowing whether particular verbs take direct or indirect objects is a notoriously complicated area, compounded by regional variations in the Spanish-speaking world concerning pronouns. The best advice is probably to learn by heart the verbs with the dependent preposition **a** given above, and remember to use the indirect object pronouns for people with them. Elsewhere, assume similarity with English if you know of no reason to think otherwise. So, as in the last question above, since in English you kiss 'someone' and you do not kiss 'to someone', assume that Spanish **besar** will take a direct object too.

Remember to have a special place in your own notes for your list of verbs with dependent prepositions to add to, as and when you come across others.

Some of the vocabulary from Day 7 on the Visual Arts and some from Day 9 on Literature will complement the vocabulary lists for today. So you will not find any terminology dealing with the visual qualities that film has in common with painting and photography, nor with the narrative element that was covered on Day 9.

---

la pantalla screen, BUT also lampshade (think of it screening the light)

la pantalla grande the big screen

la pequeña pantalla the small screen (i.e. TV) – (note how adjective position differs for these two terms)

la estrella star (in general, but including filmstar)

estrellarse to smash (think of the roughly star-like shape of the fragments)

el estrellamar starfish

el cine cinema (place and genre)

el guión screenplay, script

el guionista scriptwriter

guiar to guide

la guía guide (as in book), directory

la guía de teléfonos telephone directory

el/la guía guide (person)

---

1 Guess *cinematography*: _ _   _ _ _ _ _ _ _ _ _ _ _ _ _ _

2 And *cinematographic*: _ _ _ _ _ _ _ _ _ _ _ _ _ _ _ _

3 And *cinematic*: _ _ _ _ _ _ _ _ _ _

---

el reparto the cast (-list)

el reparto de premios prize-giving

repartir to share out, deal (cards)

el cine mudo silent films

el cine hablado talkies

el/la director/-ora director, as well as headmaster/-mistress

dirigir to direct (a film as well as in general)

en directo live (of broadcast)

los subtítulos subtitles

---

4 Guess *to subtitle*: _ _ _ _ _ _ _ _ _ _

los titulares the news headlines

doblar to dub (a film), to fold (e.g. a sheet), to double (a number), to toll (of church bell) and many other meanings.

una película doblada al inglés a film dubbed into English (note the preposition)

desdoblar to unfold, to split (a picture into two)

el/la doble double, stand-in

la música de fondo background music

tener buen fondo to be a good person deep-down, to have one's heart in the right place

el cartel poster

en cartelera showing now

la película film (at cinema), BUT ALSO to go in a still camera and in general

de película fabulous

la película de miedo horror film

la censura censorship, BUT ALSO censure

censurar to censor, BUT ALSO to censure

el/la censor/-ora censor

---

5 Thinking back to the vocabulary you learnt for geography, guess how you say *a Western:*

una película del _ _ _ _ _

6 The other term for a Western is *a cowboy film* in English and Spanish. Thinking back to the vocabulary for clothes and remembering the word for jeans that meant *cowboys*, can you work it out? If you're stuck, start by thinking of the word for *cow*.

una película de _ _ _ _ _ _ _ **s**

---

una película prohibida para menores de 18 años film rated '18'

una película de dibujos animados cartoon

la secuencia sequence

la consecuencia consequence

a consecuencia de as a result of

consecuente consistent, important (cf. 'a man of consequence')

el público audience

la publicidad publicity, advertising

publicar (spelling changes needed – see Day 24) to publish, to advertise (in sense of indiscreetly spreading information, e.g. **Estoy encinta pero**

no lo publiques, por favor I'm pregnant, but please keep it to yourself / please don't advertise the fact)

These words have already appeared but serve to remind you of their application to a cinematic context:

el estreno opening-night at theatre, premiere for film

el primer plano foreground of a painting, a close-up in still or cinema photography

And here at last is one you do not need to learn, because you already know it:

el flashback

When you think you know this vocabulary, spot-check by filling in the following wordfit puzzle. Articles are given with all nouns and counted in to the number of letters. For example, if the answer were **el gato**, it would be listed under 6 letters and the clue would be 'cat'. Score one point for every completely correct answer that you did not have to look back to the list to find.

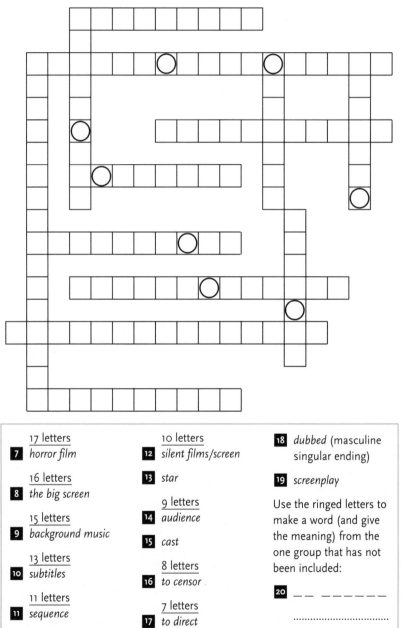

17 letters
7 horror film

16 letters
8 the big screen

15 letters
9 background music

13 letters
10 subtitles

11 letters
11 sequence

10 letters
12 silent films/screen

13 star

9 letters
14 audience

15 cast

8 letters
16 to censor

7 letters
17 to direct

18 dubbed (masculine singular ending)

19 screenplay

Use the ringed letters to make a word (and give the meaning) from the one group that has not been included:

20 _ _ _ _ _ _ _ _

....

The last exercise selects more words from the lists above, but away from the cinema context. It also revises some of the dependent prepositions from yesterday.

---

21 – 22 Si no te acuerdas _ _ su número de teléfono, consulta _ _
_ _ _ _ .

If you can't remember her telephone number, look it up in the book.

23 – 24 Arturo estaba _ _ _ _ _ _ _ _ _ _ _ _ los naipes; jugábamos
_l póquer, como de costumbre.

Arturo was dealing; we were playing poker, as usual.

25 – 26 Al sacarlo de la nevera, dejé caer un huevo que _ _ _ _ _ _ _ _ _ _
contra las baldosas. – Se _ _ pagaré de mi propio dinero – dije a la
patrona cuando me riñó.

*As I was taking it out of the fridge, I dropped an egg which smashed on the
tiled floor. 'I'll pay you for it out of my own money' I said to the boss when
she told me off.*

27 – 28 El camarero _ _ _ _ _ las servilletas, quejándose _ _ la falta
de propina.

The waiter folded the napkins, complaining about the lack of a tip.

29 – ¿Me dejas el periódico? Quiero echar un vistazo a _ _ _
_ _ _ _ _ _ _ _ _ .

*'Lend me the newspaper, will you? I'd like to have a quick look at the
headlines.'*

30 He comprado una lámpara con _ _ _ _ _ _ _ _ malva, para
hacer juego con las cortinas.

I've bought a lamp with a mauve shade to match the curtains.

Even though irregular verbs have to be learnt individually, the more you know already, the easier it becomes to recognize the similarities that there are in the irregularities. You can maximize the speed, efficiency, and accuracy of your learning by thinking of irregular verbs as patterns. This is what the exercises for today are designed to help you do.

Once you are confident that you can produce the verb-form you are looking for quickly and correctly, you will avoid losing a good many marks in an examination, and you will sound much more convincing when you are using your Spanish in real life.

I Irregular stress in the preterite

Probably the single most common irregular verb mistake seen by examiners is one that can easily be eliminated here and now. A number of key verbs with an irregular preterite have a different stress pattern in the first- and third-person singular from that of regular verbs.

Compare:

hablé, habló; comí, comió; viví, vivió – they are regular, with stress on the ending, and **dije, dijo; vine, vino; tuve, tuvo** – which are irregular, with stress on the stem.

Read them aloud and make sure you are making the correct distinction in your pronunciation, because that will help you. Because these irregular verb-forms are stressed on the stem, they do not need to have a written accent. Remember the basic rule, that words ending in a vowel are stressed on the penultimate syllable. So if you are one of the persistent offenders who writes **'dijó'**, STOP NOW!

Correct the accents on the first- and third-person singular preterite forms in the following sentences. There will be a mixture of regular and irregular verbs. Some accents will be correct – just tick these; others need crossing out, while others need to be added. Imagine you are checking through your own Spanish.

---

1 –Vamos al cine – dijó Francisco.
   'Let's go to the pictures', said Francisco.

2 Vivió hasta la edad de noventa y nueve años.
   He lived to the age of ninety-nine.

> **3**   No supe la verdad hasta mucho más tarde.
> *I didn't find out the truth until years later.*
>
> **4**–**5**   El guión se escribio en 1964, pero la película no salio hasta 1967.
> *The screenplay was written in 1964, but the film didn't come out until 1967.*
>
> **6**   El director nos pusó en primera fila cuando fuimos al estreno.
> *The director put us in the front row when we went to the premiere.*

II   -eer verbs which add a -y-
For example:
>   **creer** [to believe]
>   **leer** [to read]

The **-y-** appears only in the following forms:

▶ gerund/present participle: **creyendo, leyendo**

▶ third-persons singular and pural of the preterite: **creyó, leyó, creyeron, leyeron**
Note that in spite of the added **-y-**, these verbs still have the stress pattern of regular verbs in the preterite. So the stress falls on the ending in the first- and third-person singular forms: **creí, creyó** is just like **viví, vivió**, as far as stress is concerned.

▶ because the imperfect subjunctive is formed from the third-person plural of the preterite, the **-y-** appears all the way through the imperfect subjunctive:
>   **creyera, creyeras, creyera, creyéramos, creyerais, creyeran;**
>   **leyera, leyeras, leyera, leyéramos, leyerais, leyeran.**

Lastly, remember that **crear** [to create] is a regular **-ar** verb that has nothing to do with **creer**. Do not muddle the two even though by coincidence they can look and sound identical in certain forms, for example, **creo** [I believe/I create]. (Think how many English words look or sound identical even though they have different meanings!)

III Verbs which are regular except for their past participle
For example:
>   **abrir** [to open] – **abierto**
>   **escribir** [to write] – **escrito**
>   **imprimir** [to print] – **impreso**
>   **morir** (radical-changing and 2nd pattern, as **mentir**) [to die] – **muerto**
>   **pudrir** [to rot] – **podrido**
>   **resolver** (radical-changing) [to resolve] – **resuelto**
>   **romper** [to break] – **roto**
>   **volver** (radical-changing) [to return] – **vuelto**

Don't learn more than you have to:

▶ It is pointless to learn the whole of verbs like these which only have an irregularity in one form.

▶ There is no need to learn derivatives separately, so if a verb is the same as one of these except for a prefix, you can assume it will function in the same way. There are, unfortunately, exceptions to this rule: for example, the past participle of **corromper** [to corrupt] is regular: **corrompido**. However, it works much more often than it lets you down, so it is a reasonable rule to follow.

---

7 What is the past participle of **describir** *to describe:* _ _ _ _ _ _ _ _

8 **devolver** *to return s.th.:* _ _ _ _ _ _ _ _

revolver *to rummage:* _ _ _ _ _ _ _ _

envolver *to wrap:* _ _ _ _ _ _ _ _

desenvolver *to unwrap, unfold:* _ _ _ _ _ _ _ _ _ _ _

9 Guess what the past participle of **desenvolver** means when applied to

someone's personality: ....

IV **Verbs ending –ucir**
For example:
   conducir [to drive]   **reducir** [to reduce]
   deducir [to deduce]   **traducir** [to translate]
   inducir [to induce]

An occasional verb ending in **-ucir** will not follow the usual pattern in every respect. For example, **lucirse** [to make a spectacle of oneself] and its derivatives like **relucir** [to gleam] are regular in the preterite. But even this exception only lets you down in one tense, so it is a reasonable rule of thumb to assume that verbs ending in **-ucir** will behave like the ones listed above.

The irregularities are as follows:

i) Present indicative
     conduzco (first-person singular only; the rest is regular)

ii) Present subjunctive
     conduzca   **conduzcamos**
     conduzcas   **conduzcáis**
     conduzca   **conduzcan**

iii) Preterite
This has an irregular verb stress pattern in the first- and third-persons singular, i.e. the stress is on the stem here, so no written accent is required.

Note also how the third-person plural ending drops the -i- not -ieron, but -eron:

conduje	condujimos
condujiste	condujisteis
condujo	condujeron

iv) Imperfect subjunctive
This is formed as usual from the third-person plural of the preterite.

condujera	condujéramos
condujeras	condujerais
condujera	condujeran

When you think you know these, practise the following without looking back.

10 Write out the imperfect subjunctive of **traducir**:

(yo) trad _ _ _ _ _

(tú) trad _ _ _ _ _ _

(él/ella) trad _ _ _ _ _

(nosotros) trad _ _ _ _ _ _ _ _

(vosotros) trad _ _ _ _ _ _ _

(ellos/ellas) trad _ _ _ _ _ _

11 Write out the preterite of **reducir**:

(yo) red _ _ _

(tú) red _ _ _ _ _ _

(él/ella) red _ _ _

(nosotros) red _ _ _ _ _ _

(vosotros) red _ _ _ _ _ _ _ _

(ellos/ellas) red _ _ _ _ _ _

12 Write out the present subjunctive of **deducir**:

(yo) ded _ _ _ _

(tú) ded _ _ _ _ _

(él/ella) ded _ _ _ _

(nosotros) ded _ _ _ _ _ _ _

(vosotros) ded _ _ _ _ _ _

(ellos/ellas) ded _ _ _ _ _

Check your answers against the answer section. Only score a mark if you make no mistakes at all (including accents).

V   Other verbs featuring an irregular -j- in the preterite too.
For example:
  decir [to say] – dije . . .
  traer [to bring] – traje . . .

These boast an irregular -g- in their present tenses, which differentiates them from the -ucir group with their -zc- peculiarities. But they are helpfully similar in the preterite. Notice how verbs which are irregular in the first-person singular of the present indicative often have the same irregularity running right through their present subjunctive. This was true of the -ucir verbs with their -zc- in the present indicative first-person singular being retained through the present subjunctive. It is also true of the many irregular verbs – **decir** and **traer** among them – that have a -g- in their first-person singular of the present indicative:

i)   Present indicative

digo	decimos	**traigo** (only the first-person singular is irregular)
dices	decís	
dice	dicen	

ii) Present subjunctive

diga	digamos	traiga	traigamos
digas	digáis	traigas	traigáis
diga	digan	traiga	traigan

  Notice how the behaviour of the -e- in the stem of **decir** is reminiscent of the third pattern of radical-changing verbs (**pedir**, etc.) in the present tenses.

iii) Future

diré	diremos	(**traer** is regular)
dirás	diréis	
dirá	dirán	

(If you know the expression **el qué dirán**, meaning 'gossip-mongering', 'what the neighbours will say', it will help you remember this irregular future of **decir**.)

iv) Gerund/present participle
   diciendo (cf. **pidiendo**)   **trayendo** (cf. **creyendo** and **leyendo**)

v) Past participle
   dicho   **traído**

('**Dicho sea de paso**' will remind you of this one. Also **¡Dicho y hecho!** [No sooner said than done!] will remind you of the similarity of pattern in this form between **decir** and **hacer**.)

vi) Preterite
   Like **-ucir** verbs above, note the irregular verb stress pattern in the first- and third-persons singular, i.e. the stress is on the stem here, so no written accent is required. Note also, again like the **-ucir** group, how the third-person plural ending drops the **-i-**: not **-ieron**, but **-eron**.

dije	dijimos	traje	trajimos
dijiste	dijisteis	trajiste	trajisteis
dijo	dijeron	trajo	trajeron

Basing yourself on the third-person plural of the preterite, write out the imperfect subjunctive of **decir** and **traer**.

13 (yo)	dij _ _ _	traj _ _ _
(tú)	dij _ _ _ _	traj _ _ _ _
(él/ella)	dij _ _ _	traj _ _ _
(nosotros)	dij _ _ _ _ _ _	traj _ _ _ _ _ _
(vosotros)	dij _ _ _ _ _	traj _ _ _ _ _
(ellos/ellas)	dij _ _ _ _	traj _ _ _ _

Score one point if you get both completely right.

VI **Combinations of already familiar patterns of irregularity**
For example:
   caer [to fall]
   oír [to hear]

i) These two verbs have a -g- in some of the present forms.

> **14** Without looking back, guess where the -g- will appear, based on **decir** and **traer**:
>
> ....

ii) They have an -i- in the stem of some of the present forms.

Basing yourself on **traer** (but without looking back), try to write out the present tenses of **caer**:

15	Present indicative	Present subjunctive
(yo)	ca _ _ _	ca _ _ _
(tú)	ca _ _	ca _ _ _ _
(él/ella)	ca _	ca _ _ _
(nosotros)	ca _ _ _ _	ca _ _ _ _ _ _
(vosotros)	ca _ _ _	ca _ _ _ _ _
(ellos/ellas)	ca _ _	ca _ _ _ _

iii) They have a -y- in some of their forms.

> **16** Guess where the -y- will appear in **caer**, based on **leer** and **creer**.
>
> ....

In **oír** the -y- appears in the same places as above, plus in a few more in the present indicative:

oigo	oímos
oyes	oís
oye	oyen

VII Verbs with a -u- in the preterite
For example:

tener [to have] – **tuve**	**caber** [to fit] – **cupe**
estar [to be] – **estuve**	**saber** [to know] – **supe**
andar [to walk] – **anduve**	**haber** [to have, as the auxiliary] – **hube**
	poder [to be able] – **pude**

Try chanting these preterites aloud in the order they appear here: the rhyme patterns will help you remember them. Keep thinking about the stress on the penultimate syllable as you say them.

Practise the irregular patterns covered so far, by filling in the following list. Try to learn the patterns beforehand, so that this exercise can be a self-test done as accurately but as quickly as possible, without looking anything up in the first instance. When you have finished as much as you can, and checked thoroughly, add up your score, giving yourself 1 point for every completely correct answer. Then put right any errors and fill in any gaps. Then rewrite any that you feel shaky on, several times if necessary, until you are confident that you can produce the right answer on demand.

---

17 **(yo) decir** (pret.): _ _ _ _

18 **(tú) poder** (pret.): _ _ _ _ _ _ _

19 **(él) oír** (pret.): _ _ _

20 **(ella) retraer** *to retract* (pres. subj.): _ _ _ _ _ _ _ _ _

21 **(Vd.) maldecir** *to curse* (pres.): _ _ _ _ _ _ _ _

22 **(nosotros) deducir** *to deduce* (pres. subj.): _ _ _ _ _ _ _ _·_ _ _

23 **(vosotros) releer** *to reread* (imp. subj.): _ _ _ _ _ _ _ _ _ _

24 **(ellos) caer** (imp. subj.): _ _ _ _ _ _ _ _

25 **(ellas) andar** (pret.): _ _ _ _ _ _ _ _ _ _

26 **(Vds) creer** (gerund): _ _ _ _ _ _ _ _

VIII 'New' spellings

Spanish spelling was modernized in 1959. Among other things, the accents that used to be on **fui**, **fue**, **di**, **dio**, **vi**, **vio** were all removed. This is consistent with the stress rules practised on Day 8. If you have old editions of Spanish books you may still see the old spellings, but you should not use the accents yourself.

IX   Confusing first- and third-person endings

Do you confuse **fui** with **fue**? If you do, remember that the one that ends with **-i** is the 'I' form and the one that ends with **-e** is the 's/he' form. If you make the same mistake with the pairs for **dar** and **ver**, you can remember that you still have the **-i** ending for the 'I' form. **Dio** and **vio** should be easier because they sound like all the regular **-er** and **-ir** third-person endings in the preterite, such as **comió** and **vivió**.

To consolidate this and perhaps break a long-standing habit, fill the gaps with the right preterite form of **ser**, **ir**, **dar**, or **ver**. *Remember:* no accents!

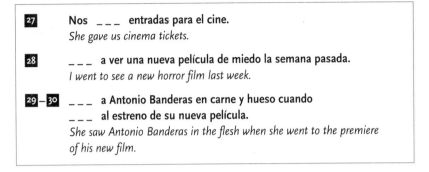

27   Nos _ _ _ entradas para el cine.
She gave us cinema tickets.

28   _ _ _ a ver una nueva película de miedo la semana pasada.
I went to see a new horror film last week.

29 – 30   _ _ _ a Antonio Banderas en carne y hueso cuando
_ _ _ al estreno de su nueva película.
She saw Antonio Banderas in the flesh when she went to the premiere of his new film.

Optional extras

If you have found it helpful to look at patterns of irregularity in verb forms as this section has done, you can build on the small selection given here by adding to your own notes. For example, **hacer** [to do/make] was not covered here, but it has the **-g-** pattern in the present tenses and you could match it with **decir** for the **-i-** in the preterite and its irregular future.

The other area you could build on would be gradually to memorize the exceptions to the derivatives rule. The only one mentioned in this section was **corromper** which does not have the same irregularity in its past participle as **romper**, but there are more. You could start making a list of them as you come across them. Here are just two more for now: **bendecir** [to bless] and **maldecir** [to curse] follow **decir** except in the future (**bendeciré** etc., and the past participle for use in compound tenses (**he bendecido** [I have blessed] etc.). If you want to use 'blessed' or 'accursed' as adjectives, there are special ones: **bendito** and **maldito**.

Finally, you may have noticed that irregular imperative forms have not been mentioned here. That is because the whole of Day 26 will be devoted to the imperative and its irregular forms will be covered there.

This is a useful area to know i) because you are studying yourself and are likely to be asked about it; ii) to find out about equivalent studies in the Spanish-speaking world; and iii) because education is always a hot political topic and a live social issue.

> **la escuela** school (in most senses of the word, excepting whales!)
> **en la escuela** at school (note the preposition and the article in Spanish; (cf. **en la universidad** at university; **en la cárcel** in prison; **en la iglesia** at church)

---

1 Guess *primary school:* _ _   _ _ _ _ _ _ _   _ _ _ _ _ _ _ _

---

la escuela nocturna night school
la escuela normal teacher training college
escolar adj. for school (as in **los niños en edad escolar** children of school age)

el/la profesor/-ora teacher (all levels, but especially above primary level)
el/la profesor/-ora particular private teacher (cf. **dar clases particulares** to give private lessons)
el profesorado teaching staff (collective term)

---

2 Guess *profession.* (*Hint:* For the gender and the stress, think of other words with a similar ending: for example, how would you say 'an argument'?)
_ _   _ _ _ _ _ _ _ _

---

la clase class, lesson (at school, e.g. **En la clase de geografía hoy** . . .) In the geography lesson today . . .), type (as in **¿Qué clase de hombre es?** What type of man is he?)
faltar a clase to miss school
salir (irreg.) **de clase** to come out of school
dar clase to teach, lecture
el/la compañero/-a de clase schoolfriend, classmate (cf. **el/la compañero/-a de piso** flatmate

3 Guess *to classify* (also *to sort*): _ _ _ _ _ _ _ _ _ _ _

la lección very limited use relative to 'lesson' in English. (Used for 'chapter' in textbook designed to be covered in one lesson; or can refer to the total of work covered, or set, in a lesson.)

repasar la lección to revise one's notes from a particular lesson

aleccionar to lecture (in the sense of 'sermonize at')

la lectura a piece of reading (reading in the general sense) (NB false friend: not 'a lecture')

hacer novillos to play truant
el novillo young bull
el/la novillero/-a learner bullfighter (who fights young bulls)

la facultad faculty, university

ausente absent
ausentarse to absent, excuse oneself
el ausentismo truancy, absenteeism

el instituto secondary school (state sector)
la institución institution
instituir to institute (conjugate as **construir**)

el colegio secondary school (private or state sector), college
el colegio de monjas convent (school) (**la monja** nun)
el colegio de curas, benedictinos, etc. Catholic boys' school (**el cura** priest; **el benedictino** Benedictine monk)
el colegial, la colegiala schoolboy, schoolgirl
el/la colega colleague

4 Guess *mental faculties*: _ _ _   _ _ _ _ _ _ _ _ _ _ _
_ _ _ _ _ _ _ _

la universidad university
universitario adj. for university (e.g. **el sector universitario** the university sector)

5 Guess *the universe*: _ _   _ _ _ _ _ _ _ _
6 Guess *universal*: _ _ _ _ _ _ _ _ _ _

el/la estudiante student
estudiantil adjective for 'student' (e.g. **la vida estudiantil** student life)
estudiar to study, learn (by studying, as in to learn a language, a musical

instrument, etc.), to work (when used for studying, e.g. **Tendrás que estudiar mucho si quieres aprobar los exámenes** You'll have to work hard if you want to pass your exams)
el estudio studio, study

7 Guess *studious:* _ _ _ _ _ _ _ _ _

---

el/la alumno/-a pupil, student (in the   el/la alumno/-a externo/-a day pupil
    sense of 'pupil')   el/la alumno/-a interno/-a boarder
el/la antiguo/-a alumno/-a old boy/girl

Fill the gaps.

8 – 9 ¿Cuántos _ _ _ _ _ _ _   _ _ _ _ _ _ _ _   hay en este
_ _ _ _ _ _ _?
How many boarders are there at this school?

10 – 12 _ _   _ _ _ _   _ _ _ _ _ _ _ _ _ _ _ _   consiste _ _
más que _ _ _ _ _ _ _ _ _ .
Student life consists of more than studying.

13 – 14 Se _ _   _ _ _ _ _ _ _ _ _ _ _   un nuevo sistema según el
cual _ _ _   _ _ _ _ _ _ _ _ _ _ _ _   no sabrán de quiénes son
los exámenes que están corrigiendo.
*A new system has been instituted whereby the lecturers won't know whose
scripts they are marking.*

15 En los últimos años mi pobre abuelo ha perdido sus
_ _ _ _ _ _ _ _ _ _   _ _ _ _ _ _ _ _   casi por completo.
*In recent years my poor grandfather has almost completely lost his mental
faculties.*

16 – 17 De jóvenes, yo y un par de _ _ _ _ _ _ _ _ _ _ _   _ _
_ _ _ _   _ _ _ _ _ _ _ _   _ _ _ _ _ _ _ _   todos los
miércoles por la tarde para evitar la clase de química.
*When we were young, a couple of schoolfriends and I used to play truant
every Wednesday afternoon, to avoid our chemistry lesson.*

18 – 19 No suele haber uniforme en _ _ _   _ _ _ _ _ _ _ _ _ _
pero sí en _ _ _   _ _ _ _ _ _ _ _ _   _ _   _ _ _ _ _ _ _ .
There isn't usually a uniform at state secondary schools but there is at convents.

20 Invitan a _ _ _   _ _ _ _ _ _ _ _ _   _ _ _ _ _ _ _   a una
cena de reunión todos los diez años.
Old boys and girls are invited to a reunion dinner once every ten years.

21 Después de _ _   _ _ _ _ _ _ _ _ _ _ _ _ , ¿a qué piensas
dedicarte?
What line of work do you think you'll go in for after university?

22 Estaba _ _ _ _ _ _ _   cuando nos explicó _ _   _ _ _ _ _ _ _
14, pero _ _ estudié en casa después.
I was absent when he taught Lesson 14, but I worked on it at home afterwards.

el curso academic year, year of study (as in **estudiantes de primer curso** first-year students)

cursar estudios to study (at university level)

en el decurso de los años in the course of/over the years

corregir (radical-changing, third pattern, as **pedir**), to correct, mark

incorregible incorrigible

el corregidor formerly a judge/mayor (to be found, for example, in Golden Age drama)

suspender to fail (exams, assessment), to suspend

el suspenso fail

las notas results, marks

anotar to annotate

notar to be noticeable, to be able to tell

el horario timetable

a deshora out of hours, at a surprising or inconvenient time

¡enhorabuena! congratulations!

¡Ya era hora! about time too! (takes the subjunctive if followed by a verb, e.g. **Ya era hora de que llegaras** It was about time you got here)

pasar un examen to take an examination (NB false friend: <u>not</u> 'to pass it')

repasar to revise

el repaso revision session, course

aprobar (un examen) (radical-changing) to pass (an exam)

un aprobado a straight pass

desaprobar to disapprove of (note that there is no preposition in Spanish)

When you think you know these, try unscrambling these anagrams with the help of the context:

23 ¿Aprobaste todos tus exámenes? ¡Hanubanereo!

¡— — — — — — — — — — —!

24 ¡Cuántas veces te he dicho ya que no me ensucies el mantel con tus pinturas! ¡Y tú, ni caso! Eres libercornige.

— — — — — — — — — — —

¡Cuántas veces te he dicho ya que no me ensucies el mantel con tus pinturas! ¡Y tú, ni caso! No tienes remedio.

25 ¿Conoces este libro? Me está ayudando bastante; consiste en un aspero general de gramática enfocado en los puntos más difíciles. — — — — — —

26 En mi colegio, si te depunsens en más de tres asignaturas tienes que repetir el curso. — — — — — — — — —

27 Se querían mucho al casarse pero en el ucredos de los años su amor iba apagándose. — — — — — — —

28 Veo por la cara que pones que pseudabreas mi idea. — — — — — — — — — — —

29 Algunos profesores tardan semanas en orcigrer los deberes de sus alumnos.

— — — — — — — —

30 Te onto muy cansada; has estado estudiando toda la noche otra vez, ¿verdad?   — — — —

Remember to check your answers against the answer section. Are you still keeping up with making a note of any words or expressions that you have come across for the first time in *Upgrade?* You will maximize its usefulness if you do.

Impress your examiners by using conditional sentences

Conditional sentences are a nicely self-contained set of uses of the subjunctive. If you master the rules and add them to the easy subjunctive constructions practised on Day 3, you will start to have a good repertoire of accurate 'hits' with the subjunctive. Put that together with the work on correct verb-forms so that when you mean to use the subjunctive you get it right and you will really see a tangible step up in the level of your Spanish.

▶ The first thing is to be able recognize the type of construction that comes into the set of rules governing conditional sentences.

▶ The second is to classify the construction correctly and match it to one of the three basic types of conditional sentence.

▶ The third is then to follow the rules and produce a correct conditional sentence.

I   Identifying a conditional sentence and sorting it into one of the three basic types
Some sentences containing the word 'if' in English, and **si** in Spanish, are not conditional sentences for our purposes today, while others that do not contain 'if' are.

As the name implies, a conditional sentence makes the doing of one half of the action in the sentence conditional upon the other half. For example:

i)   If I win the lottery, I'll buy myself a new car.
    (Should I win the lottery, I'll buy myself a new car.)

ii) If I won the lottery, I'd buy myself a new car.
    (Were I to win the lottery, I'd buy myself a new car.)

iii) If I had won the lottery last week, I'd have bought myself a new car.
    (Had I won the lottery last week, I'd have bought myself a new car.)

The buying of the new car in all cases is conditional upon winning the lottery. If that condition is not met, I keep my old car. *Note* that in all three cases there are ways of expressing this which do not use the word 'if'.

Here are some uses of 'if' that are <u>not</u> like the three sentences above.

iv) 'If he was handsome, he was also rather stupid.' OR: 'He was handsome if stupid.'

Here the 'if' really means 'although'; the stupidity is not dependent on the condition of 'handsomeness' being met. If he had had an accident that had left him so badly scarred that he was not handsome any more, it would not stop him from being stupid.

v)   'When I was a child and we used to spend the holidays in Brighton, we would go to the beach if it was good weather and stay at the hotel if it was raining.'

Even though what we did was dependent on the weather, the 'ifs' really mean 'when' in a sentence of this kind. So if you can replace an 'if' either with 'although' or with 'when', without changing the meaning of the sentence, you would simply translate into Spanish in a straightforward manner:

Si era guapo, también era bastante estúpido.

Cuando era niña y pasábamos las vacaciones en Brighton, íbamos a la playa si hacía buen tiempo y nos quedábamos en el hotel si llovía.

Match the following sentences to one of the five examples discussed above. Ring the right answer.

1 If the plumber arrives after eleven o'clock, I'll be out.	i ii iii iv v
2 If you had come before eleven, I'd have been here.	i ii iii iv v
3 If we did not sit up straight at the table, our father used to tell us off.	i ii iii iv v
4 It was sunny, if there were a few clouds to be seen.	i ii iii iv v
5 If I thought you meant that, it would be extremely hurtful.	i ii iii iv v

Once you have decided that a particular sentence is one of the three basic types of conditional sentence, you have to know the formula for expressing it in Spanish:

i)   Present in the 'if' clause – future in the main clause

Note that this construction is exactly the same as English. There are no subjunctives here. (In fact, you can never have the present subjunctive after **si**.) For example:

Si me toca la lotería ['if' clause], **me compraré un nuevo coche** [main clause].

ii) Imperfect subjunctive in the 'if' clause – conditional in the main clause

Note that this is the same as formal, educated English ('If I were to win . . .', 'Were I to win . . .'), but commonly ignored in everyday usage – except, funnily enough, in the expression, 'If I were you . . .'. For example:

Si me tocara la lotería ['if' clause], **me compraría un nuevo coche** [main clause].

iii) Pluperfect subjunctive in the 'if' clause – conditional perfect in the main clause. English equivalents very rarely use any identifiable subjunctive here, alas. For example:

Si me hubiera tocado la lotería ['if' clause], **me habría comprado un nuevo coche** [main clause].

Fill in the gaps using each of the verbs from the alphabetical list once. First decide which of the three types of conditional sentence you are dealing with then follow the pattern.

---

ayudar, decir, divertirse, enfadarse, estar, llegar

6 – 7 Si me lo _ _ _ _ _ _ _ _ _ _ _ _ _ _ antes, _ _ _ _ _ _
_ _ _ _ _ _ **ayudarte.**
If you had told me sooner, I'd have been able to help you.

7 – 8 Si _ _ _ _ _ _ _ _ _ tarde, mis padres _ _
_ _ _ _ _ _ _ _ _ _ .
If we're late, my parents will get angry.

8 – 9 Si tú _ _ _ _ _ _ _ _ _ _ _ aquí ahora, ¡cuánto _ _ _
_ _ _ _ _ _ _ _ _ _ _ _ _ _ juntos!
If you were here now, we'd have such a great time together.

These basic formulae are not affected by the possibility that exists in Spanish generally of using a continuous tense (e.g. **estoy hablando**). Just make sure that you are using the continuous equivalent of the tense and mood you need. Practise using continuous tenses in the following sentences:

---

10 – 11 Si tú _ _ _ _ _ _ _ _ _ _ _ _ _ _ _ escuchando cuando te
lo explicó, no nos _ _ _ _ _ _ _ _ _ _ _ _ _ _ _ _ _ .
If you had been listening when he explained it all, we wouldn't have got lost.

12 – 13 Si yo _ _ _ _ _ tu padre, no _ _ _ _ _ _ _ _ diciéndome
cosas así.
If I were your father, you wouldn't be saying things like that to me.

14 – 15 Si _ _ _ _ _ hablando por teléfono cuando llegue yo, te
_ _ _ _ _ _ _ _ en el coche.
If you're on the phone when I arrive, I'll wait for you in the car.

In conversational Spanish, you will quite often hear other combinations of tenses and moods. If you are sufficiently confident to use these yourself when the level of informality makes them acceptable, go ahead; but if you want one safe and always correct set of formulae to use, stick to the ones you have been practising just now.

II -ra imperfect subjunctive doubling for conditional

In more standard and formal Spanish you will also come across the use of the **-ra** form of the imperfect subjunctive as an alternative for certain conditionals, notably **haber**, **poder**, and **deber**. So, **no nos habríamos perdido** in numbers 10–11 above, could have been **no nos hubiéramos perdido**, for example. It is important to understand that this construction is an alternative for the conditional – no more. You do not need to use it yourself, just to understand it when you see or hear it.

Do not confuse it with the obligatory subjunctives in the 'if' clauses and remember that in Spanish, as in English, the 'if' clause can come first or second in word order.

To make sure you are clear on the distinction between an optional and a compulsory subjunctive, ring the right answer below, deciding whether the underlined verb is an optional alternative to the conditional, or the compulsory subjunctive. To get the answer right, all you have to do is look where the conditional falls in the sentence: if it is in the 'if' clause it will be compulsory (C); if it is in the main clause, it will be optional (O).

16 **Te lo hubiera explicado si me hubieras dado la ocasión.** *I'd have explained if you had given me the chance.*	C	O
17 **Si ganara un dineral, te lo daría todo.** *If I won a fortune, I'd give it all to you.*	C	O
18 **No hubiéramos escogido ese color grisáceo si nos hubieran dicho que ya estaba pasado de moda.** *We wouldn't have chosen that greyish colour if we'd been told it was out of fashion now.*	C	O

III Same-subject infinitive constructions

You may have noticed that in all the conditional sentences so far, the subject of the 'if' clause has been different from the subject of the main clause. For example, in question 18, the subject of the main clause is **nosotros**, whereas the subject of the 'if' clause is **ellos**. Cast your eye over the other conditional sentences and check you can see the same difference in subject for each.

If you need to use a conditional sentence where the subject is the same in both clauses, you can use an infinitive construction instead of the 'if' clause, thus avoiding the obligatory subjunctives. These infinitive constructions are both easy to use and elegant in form. For example, to say, 'If I had known, I wouldn't have done it', the subject is 'I' in both clauses, so you can say:

De haberlo sabido, no lo habría hecho.

Try these:

> **19** **Lo habrías odiado, de** _ _ _ _ _   _ _ _ _ _ _.
> *You would have hated it, had you been there.*
>
> **20** **De** _ _ _ _ _ _ _   _ _ _ _ _ _ _ _ **a tiempo, habría dicho algo.**
> *If I had remembered in time, I'd have said something.*

The best way to become confident and relaxed about using these constructions is to practise them, so here are some more gap-fillers. This time the sentences will not necessarily be one of the three types of conditional sentence – some will be the same subject type that can use the infinitive construction, while others will be the 'if'-meaning-'although' and 'if'-meaning-'when' type – so be on your guard. The verbs to use are listed before the sentences in alphabetical order.

castigar (spelling changes needed – see Day 24) to punish
decir (irregular) to tell
enfadarse to get angry
explicar (spelling changes needed – see Day 24) to explain
gustar to please
llegar (spelling changes needed – see Day 24) to arrive
reñir (radical-changing, third pattern, as **pedir**) to scold
saber (irregular) to know
ser (irregular) to be

> **21**–**22** **Si no me** _ _ _ _ _ _ _ _ _ **, te lo** _ _ _ _ _.
> *If I didn't like you, I'd tell you so.*

> *Careful:* The subject is the same for both clauses in English, but remember that in Spanish you will have to say 'If you didn't please me, I'd tell you so'.

> **23**–**24** **Teníamos que ir a misa todos los domingos, y si** _ _ _ _ _ _ _ _ _ _
> **tarde, las monjas nos** _ _ _ _ _ _ _ _ _ _ _.
> *We had to go to mass every Sunday and if we were late, the nuns would punish us.*

> *Hint:* The imperfect at the beginning of the sentence should alert you to the fact that this is talking about habitual action in the past, so the English 'would' is an alternative for 'used to'.

25 – 26 Si le _ _ _ _ _ _ _ _ por qué llegaste tarde, no te _ _ _ _ _ _ _.
If you explain why you were late, she won't tell you off.

27 – 28 De _ _ _ _ _ _ _ _ _ _ _ _ _ _ , no se _ _ _ _ _ _
_ _ _ _ _ _ _ _.
If she had known, she wouldn't have got angry.

29 – 30 _ _ _ ridículo, si _ _ _ comprensible, que les tuviéramos tanto
miedo.
It was ridiculous, if it was understandable, that we were so scared of them.

Upgrade your vocabulary: Health

The practical usefulness of this area of vocabulary is obvious, but in addition to that, health is another area of debate which, like education, is on the political agenda and a key social issue, so that a good command of the vocabulary in the field will give you access to numerous features and debates in the press and other mass media.

frío cold
resfriarse (conjugated like **continuar**) to catch cold
enfriarse (conjugated like **resfriarse**) to go cold, cool (down)
el resfriado cold (in the head)
un sudor frío a cold sweat

la fiebre fever, temperature
tener fiebre to have a temperature (note the lack of the article in Spanish)
febril feverish
la fiebre del heno hay-fever

la gripe the 'flu
tener gripe to have the 'flu (no article in Spanish again)

1 If a medicine is recommended for **estados gripales**, guess what that is:

....

la alergia allergy   **tener alergia a** to be allergic to

2 Guess *allergic:* _ _ _ _ _ _ _ _

la salud health

3 Guess *public health:* _ _ _ _ _ _ _ _ _ _ _ _ _ _

¡Salud! Cheers! Good health! (toast)
saludable healthy
saludar to say hello, greet, salute

el síndrome syndrome
el SIDA AIDS
el/la sidoso/-a person with AIDS

el cáncer cancer (illness and star sign)

---

4 Based on the **SIDA–sidoso** relationship, guess how you say *a person with cancer*:

el/la _ _ _ _ _ _ _ _ _/-a.

---

cancerígeno carcinogenic

la cirugía surgery (in the operating theatre, not doctor's consulting rooms)

Guess the meaning:

---

5 la cirugía estética: ....

---

el/la cirujano/-a surgeon
quirúrgico surgical
el quirófano operating theatre

la vacuna vaccine
vacunar to vaccinate

la anestesia anaesthetic

---

6 Guess *anaesthetist:* **el/la** _ _ _ _ _ _ _ _ _ _ _ _

7 Guess *to anaesthetize:* _ _ _ _ _ _ _ _ _ _

---

el/la practicante paramedic/nurse (often
   used to give injections, change
   dressings)
practicar (spelling changes needed –
   see Day 24) to practise
práctico practical

enfermo ill
el/la enfermero/-a nurse
enfermarse to get ill
enfermizo sickly (of person), unhealthy
   (as in e.g., obsession)
la enfermedad illness

A few miscellaneous 'unguessables'

el sarampión measles
la varicela chicken pox
la jaqueca migraine

el sarpullido rash
el infarto heart attack

When you think you know these, fill in the vocabulary dial opposite with the help of the English terms. Except in cases where the term can be masculine or feminine without changing its ending, articles are included – according to whether they apply to a man or a woman. Score half a point for each that you get completely right, without looking back to the lists. At the end, use the shaded letters to make the missing word.

8 (a) *surgery* (2,7)
   (b) *chicken pox* (2,8)

9 (a) *allergy* (2,7)
   (b) *vaccine* (2, 6)

10 (a) *anaesthetic* (2, 9)
   (b) *AIDS* (2, 4)

11 (a) *(female) nurse* (2, 9)
   (b) *anaesthetist* (11)

12 (a) *migraine* (2, 7)
   (b) *practical* (8)

13 (a) *sickly* (9)
   (b) *man with AIDS* (2, 6)

14 (a) *operating theatre* (2, 9)
   (b) *allergic* (8)

15 (a) *cancerous* (9)
   (b) *rash* (2, 10)

16 (a) *cold in the head* (2, 9)
   (b) *heart attack* (2, 7)

17 (a) *'flu* (2, 5)
   (b) *syndrome* (2, 8)

18 (a) *paramedic who gives
       injections* (11)
   (b) *healthy* (9)

19 (a) *temperature* (2, 6)

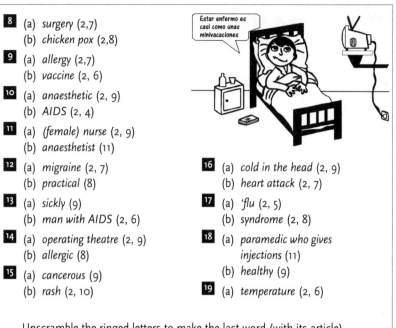

Estar enfermo es
casi como unas
minivacaciones

Unscramble the ringed letters to make the last word (with its article).
Give its meaning:

19 (b) ....

START

la seguridad social Spanish national health service (not 'social security')
la seguridad security, safety
inseguro insecure
asegurar to assure, insure, ensure

los pulmones lungs

herir (radical-changing, second pattern, as **mentir**) to wound
la herida wound
curar una herida to dress a wound

la receta prescription, recipe
recetar to prescribe

Guess the meaning:

20 la pulmonía ....

As in English, **-itis** is a suffix that can be added on to numerous words to mean an illness relating to that noun. In Spanish these words are all feminine. Guess the following:

los bronquios *bronchial tubes*

21 *bronchitis:* _ _   _ _ _ _ _ _ _ _ _ _

22 *arthritis:* _ _   _ _ _ _ _ _ _ _

23 *ear infection:* **una ot** _ _ _ _

las amígdalas *tonsils*

24 *tonsillitis:* _ _   _ _ _ _ _ _ _ _ _ _ _ _

Fill in the gaps:

25   Llevaron a los _ _ _ _ _ _ _ al hospital.
The wounded were taken to hospital.

26   ¿Cómo funciona _ _   _ _ _ _ _ _ _ _ _   _ _ _ _ _
en Inglaterra?
How does the British National Health Service work?

27, **28**   El médico me _ _ _ _ _ _ unas gotas para _ _ _ _ _ _ _ _.
The doctor prescribed some drops for my ear infection.

29   A los niños de hoy ya no se suele sacarles _ _ _
_ _ _ _ _ _ _ _.
Nowadays they don't usually take children's tonsils out.

30   Estuve un mes en la cama a causa de una _ _ _ _ _ _ _ _.
I was in bed for a month with pneumonia.

Narrative (both oral and written) can be livened up greatly by the inclusion of passages of dialogue provided that you have some stylistic and lexical variety to draw on.

ALTERNATIVES TO DECIR

The first step to upgrading your style in this area, then, is to know and use a good range of alternatives to **decir**. Here are some to make sure you have in your repertoire.

balbucear to stammer, falter

bramar to roar, bellow

chillar to scream, shriek

exclamar to exclaim

gemir (radical-changing, third pattern, as **pedir**) to whine, moan, groan

interrumpir to interrupt (takes indirect object for person)

mascullar to mutter, murmur

oponer (irregular, as **poner**) to object

preguntar to ask

proseguir (radical-changing, third pattern, as **seguir**; spelling changes needed – see Day 24) to go on

refunfuñar to grumble

replicar (spelling changes – see Day 24) to rejoin (i.e. snap back)

responder to reply

saludar to greet

susurrar to whisper (remember to pronounce that double 'r' in your head)

Make up your mind to use **decir** no more than once in any dialogue.

In the following dialogue, fill the gaps with some of the verbs above, using each verb once.

1–**7** —Buenos días – me s _ _ _ _ _ Doña Pilar, la vecina de arriba. Es una metomentodo; no me gusta nada y por lo tanto no tenía ganas de conversar con ella.
—Buenos días – le r _ s _ _ _ _ _ seco.
—¿Como está usted? – me p _ _ _ _ _ _ _ .
—Regular – m _ _ _ _ _ _ _, volviéndole la espalda para llamar el ascensor.
—¿Y su señora madre? – p _ _ _ _ _ _ _ _ _ . –¿Qué tal su artritis? Sufre tanto y no se queja nunca . . .
—Usted me disculpará – le i _ _ _ _ _ _ _ _ _ – pero tengo mucha prisa.
—Sí, sí, ya lo sé. Los jóvenes de hoy no tenéis nunca tiempo para nada – ref _ _ _ _ _ _ Doña Pilar. En aquel momento, el ascensor acabó de llegar y con un gran suspiro de alivio, me escapé de ella.

'Good morning,' Doña Pilar greeted me. She lives above us. She is an interfering woman; I don't like her at all and so I had no desire to get into conversation with her.
'Good morning','I replied rather sharply.
'How are you?' she asked.
'Not bad,' I muttered, turning my back on her to call the lift.
'And your dear mother?', she went on. 'How is her arthritis? She puts up with so much and never complains...'
'Forgive me,' I interrupted her, 'but I'm in rather a hurry.'
'Yes, yes, I know. You young people nowadays, you never have time for anything', she grumbled. At that moment, the lift finally arrived and heaving a great sigh of relief I escaped.

Practise the verbs you have not yet used in the following sentences.

8   —¡Una araña! – ch _ _ _ _ la niña.
'A spider!' screamed the little girl.

9   —Confía en mí. Sígueme pero no hagas ruido – s _ _ _ _ _ _.
'Trust me. Follow me but don't make a noise', he whispered.

10   —Me has salvado la vida; no sé cómo agradecerte – b _ _ _ _ _ _ _,
ruborizándome.
'You have saved my life; I don't know how to thank you', I stammered blushing.

11–**12**   —¡No me hables así! – b _ _ _ _
su padre.
—¡Te hablaré como me dé la real
gana! – rep _ _ _ _ la hija.
'Don't speak to me like that!'
roared her father.
'I'll speak to you however I darn
well like!' the daughter snapped
back.

13   —Tú, por aquí . . . ¡Qué coincidencia! – e _ _ _ _ _ _.
'You here, what a coincidence!' I exclaimed.

14   —No aguanto más, no aguanto más – g _ _ _ _.
'I can't take any more, I can't take any more', she moaned.

15   —Por favor, déjame ir a la fiesta. Volveré en taxi después.
—Y ¿si no hay? – o _ _ _ _ mi madre.
'Please let me go to the party. I'll come back by taxi afterwards.'
'And what if there aren't any?' my mother objected.

ADVERB AVOIDANCE
In English, adverbs are commonly added to a verb used to describe a character's manner of speaking: for example, 'he replied smilingly, crossly', and so on.
Remember that Spanish uses adverbs less widely than English and so if you want your Spanish to sound as natural as possible, try to find an alternative to an adverb each time you want to use one. It would be a mistake to go too far and never use an adverb in Spanish, but reducing the number you use by having some alternatives to hand will be of benefit to your style. Here are some ideas:

i) A noun phrase will sometimes work: for example, **respondió con una sonrisa**, would be a good way of handling 'he replied smilingly'.

ii) An adjective in Spanish can often replace an adverb in English: **respondió enfadado** would be a sensible choice for 'he replied crossly'.

iii) A present participle will sometimes work: **respondió sonriendo** would be an alternative to i).

iv) If an English adverb relates to the tone of voice, you can say so explicitly in Spanish. For example, '. . . he said hoarsely', could be . . . **dijo con voz ronca**. Note especially **a media voz** and **en voz baja**, both for 'quietly'. Of the two, select **a media voz** if there is room for ambiguity, since **en voz baja** also means 'silently', as in **leer en voz baja**, 'to read to oneself'.

Use one of these adverb-avoidance strategies in the following sentences. Choose the most appropriate one for the context from the list and try to find an equivalent adverb in English.

---

con resentimiento   con voz trémula   incrédulo   riendo

16   —¡No me digas! – exclamó _ _ _ _ _ _ _ _ _ .

'You don't say!' he exclaimed ....

17   —¿Por qué me toca siempre a mí? – replicó _ _ _
_ _ _ _ _ _ _ _ _ _ _ _.
'Why is it always my turn?' he rejoined ....

18   —No me atrevo – confesó _ _ _   _ _ _   _ _ _ _ _ _ _.

'I dare not', she confessed ....

19   —¡Claro que no me importa! – respondió _ _ _ _ _ _.

'Of course I don't mind!' she answered ....

INVERSION

Remember that the inversion that is still used in English for direct speech, but which is sounding more and more old-fashioned now, is obligatory in Spanish. For example:

'Good morning,' Mrs Pérez said / said Mrs Pérez.
has to be
–Buenos días – dijo la Sra. Pérez.

It cannot be **la Sra. Pérez dijo**.

EXTRA PRONOUNS

Remember too that object pronouns are included in Spanish more than in English. For example, in English you might have:

'Come here!' I said. 'No!' he replied.
BUT it would be a good idea to add object pronouns in Spanish:
   –¡Ven aquí! – le dije. –¡No! – me respondió.

Correct and polish the following dialogue, as if it were your own work produced in an examination. It is printed with extra wide line-spacing, so that you can cross out words and write above them. Give yourself one point for each time you

▶ remove a repetitious use of **decir**;   ▶ replace adverbs with alternatives; and
▶ add object pronouns;   ▶ correct forgotten inversions.

Here are some extra verbs you might like to work in:

agregar (spelling changes needed – see Day 24) to add **añadir** to add	**contestar** an option for 'to reply' **interponer** (as **poner**) to interject, put in	**interrumpirse** to interrupt oneself, to break off to say **comentar** to comment

There might be mistakes in the verb-forms too, so check them as you go along as well.

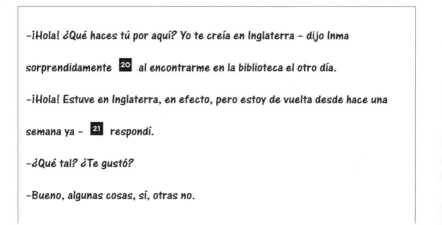

–¡Hola! ¿Qué haces tú por aquí? Yo te creía en Inglaterra – dijo Inma

sorprendidamente **20** al encontrarme en la biblioteca el otro día.

–¡Hola! Estuve en Inglaterra, en efecto, pero estoy de vuelta desde hace una

semana ya – **21** respondí.

–¿Qué tal? ¿Te gustó?

–Bueno, algunas cosas, sí, otras no.

–¿Por ejemplo? – Inma 22 dijó 23 .

–El tiempo, claro que no me gustó; llovió casi todos los días. En cambio, me

encantó Londres: las tiendas, los monumentos . . .

–¿Y los londinenses? – dijo 24 Inma sonrientemente 25 .

–En realidad no conocí a muchos. En la escuela de idiomas éramos todos

extranjeros, desde luego, y los profesores se marchaban en seguida después de

las clases. Pero viví con una familia inglesa bastante simpática.

–Y ahora hablas perfectamente el inglés, supongo – dije 26 Inma

sarcásticamente 27 .

–¡Qué va! – yo 28 dije. –Pero me lo pasé muy bien. Deberías hacerlo tú.

¿Quieres que te dé la dirección de la escuela de idiomas?

–Sí, gracias. Oye – dijo 29 . –Tengo que irme. Hasta pronto.

–Adiós, Inma – y luego dije 30 –Y cuando tengas más tiempo, te enseñaré las

fotos que saqué en Londres.

–Perfecto. Adiós.

Check your answers in the answer section. The maximum you can score is 11 points.

Make the most of the logic of Spanish spelling

*Notwithstanding a few irritants like the silent **h**, Spanish spelling is wonderfully logical, much more so than English. It is therefore possible to learn some key spelling rules and apply them across the board, rather than have to learn how to spell myriads of individual words. This is particularly useful in conjugating verbs, since many can be taken out of the irregular category – requiring individual memorization – and simply treated as regular verbs which demand some spelling changes here and there. This is because you can safely assume that the sound at the end of the stem of a regular verb will not change as you conjugate it, so if the spelling needs adjustment to maintain that, go ahead.*

The verbs involved are the ones whose stems end in a letter which is either pronounced differently according to the letter that follows it, or it never appears unless it has to. The stem endings are therefore: **c**, **g**, **gu**, **qu** and **z**.

I   /k/

If the ending of the stem is a hard **c** (as in **casa**), it will have to become **qu** to keep it sounding the same, whenever the ending starts with **e** or **i**.

For example, **tocar** will have to change the **c** to **qu** in the first-person singular of the preterite: **toqué**. Otherwise, the **c** would sound soft, as in **cero**. The same will be necessary all the way through the present subjunctive: **toque, toques, toque**, etc.

II   /g/

To keep a **g** hard (as in **gordo**) at the end of a stem, a different strategy is employed, namely, the addition of a silent **u**.

So, for example, **llegar** will need it in the first-person singular of the preterite, **llegué** – and again, right through the present subjunctive: **llegue, llegues, llegue**, etc.

Where the stem of an **-ir** verb ends in a hard /g/ sound, the reverse pattern will be found: it will need the **u** in the infinitive and lose it in the forms where it is not needed.

Seguir, for example, is not really an irregular verb. It is third pattern radical-changing (like **pedir**) and it keeps its **u** only where it needs to for the **g** to remain hard. Thus, it is not needed in the first-person singular of the present indicative: **sigo**, or in the present subjunctive: **siga, sigas, siga**, etc.

III   - /Θ/

Where a verb stem ends in /Θ/ (a soft **c** as in **cero**), it will have to be spelt with a **z** to keep the sound the same, when the ending begins with **a** or **o**. If it is an **-ar** verb, that means the infinitive will have a **z**. For example: **cazar** [to hunt] is **cacé** in the first-person singular of the preterite and right through the present subjunctive: **cace, caces, cace**, etc. For **-er** and **-ir** verbs, the infinitive will have a **c**, but become **z** where necessary.

Write out the forms:

> **1**   Where will the **c** at   _ _ _ _ _   _ _ _ _ _ _ _ _
> the end of **vencer**
> _to defeat_ need to   _ _ _ _ _ _   _ _ _ _ _ _ _
> become a **z**?   _ _ _ _ _ _   _ _ _ _ _ _
>
>   _ _ _ _ _

Zurcir [to darn] will behave in the same fashion.

IV   /x/

The spelling of /x/ (the soft **g** sound, as in **gesto** and **jamón**) is a little less logical because a **j** does not automatically become a **g** wherever possible. Whereas a **z** becomes a **c** whenever it can (with a very few exceptions), a **j** will stay a **j** at the end of a regular verb stem. For example, **bajar** [to descend] never changes its **j** into a **g**.

On the other hand, a verb stem ending in the same sound, but spelt with a **g**, will have to change to a **j** to keep itself soft with certain endings. For example, **coger** [to take] will have to use a **j** in the first-person singular of the present indicative: **cojo** and all the way through the present subjunctive: **coja, cojas, coja**, etc. The same will arise with an **-ir** verb like **dirigir** [to direct].

Fill in the following table, paying special attention to the last sound of the stem of the verb:

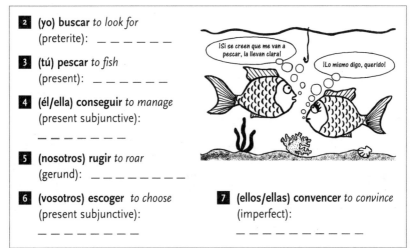

> **2**   **(yo) buscar** _to look for_
> (preterite):   _ _ _ _ _ _
>
> **3**   **(tú) pescar** _to fish_
> (present):   _ _ _ _ _ _
>
> **4**   **(él/ella) conseguir** _to manage_
> (present subjunctive):
> _ _ _ _ _ _ _ _
>
> **5**   **(nosotros) rugir** _to roar_
> (gerund):   _ _ _ _ _ _ _ _
>
> **6**   **(vosotros) escoger** _to choose_
> (present subjunctive):
> _ _ _ _ _ _ _ _ _
>
> **7**   **(ellos/ellas) convencer** _to convince_
> (imperfect):
> _ _ _ _ _ _ _ _ _ _

Speech bubbles: ¡Si se creen que me van a pescar, la llevan clara! — ¡Lo mismo digo, querido!

V /gw/

We have already seen that **g** uses a silent **u** to keep itself sounding hard when the vowel following it is one that would otherwise produce a soft pronunciation (as in **seguir**). But if a **u** follows a **g** when it is not needed to harden it, it is there in its own right and therefore pronounced. This is the case with verbs like **averiguar** [to ascertain] and **apaciguar** [to calm]. What happens to verbs like these that want the **u** to be heard when the ending happens to start with an **e**? As you probably know, the answer is to add a dieresis [ü].

Give the first-person singular of the preterite:

8 averiguar	apaciguar
— — — — — — —	— — — — — — —

VI These rules applied to words other than verbs

These rules are particularly useful to know for conjugating verbs but they are applicable to all Spanish words and, once you know them, should help you with all your spelling.

Add a dieresis where necessary to the following words, in all of which the **u** after the **g** is pronounced:

9 el agua (feminine) *water*	**12** la verguenza *shame*
10 el guisqui *whisky*	**13** el guardia *policeman*
11 la tregua *truce*	

In all of the following words, the **g** is hard. Will there need to be a **u** after it or not? Ring the right answer.

14 el geto / gueto *ghetto*	**16** el gorila / guorila *gorilla*
15 la gerrilla / guerrilla *guerilla warfare*	**17** el gijarro / guijarro *pebble*

In all of the following words there is a /Θ/ (soft **c**) sound. Basing yourself on the rule that says that **z** will automatically be replaced by **c** wherever possible, ring the right answer (the few exceptions to this rule will not appear in this exercise.)

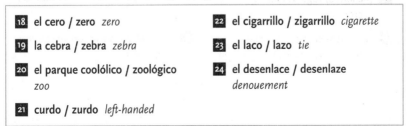

18 el cero / zero *zero*	**22** el cigarrillo / zigarrillo *cigarette*
19 la cebra / zebra *zebra*	**23** el laco / lazo *tie*
20 el parque coolólico / zoológico *zoo*	**24** el desenlace / desenlaze *denouement*
21 curdo / zurdo *left-handed*	

VII /k/ and /kw/

Because the hard **c** sound has **qu** to use where necessary, there is no such thing as a silent **u** after a **c**: **cu** is always pronounced /kw/ and **qu** is never pronounced /kw/ or used at all if a **c** will be pronounced /k/.

In each of the following words the pronounciation will be given first, either as /k/ or /kw/. Based on that, ring the right spelling:

25 /k/ **el cueso / queso**
cheese

28 /kw/ **la cualidad / qualidad**
quality

26 /kw/ **la cuestión / questión**
issue

29 /k/ **Cuito / Quito**
Quito (capital of Ecuador)

27 /kw/ **¿cuánto? / ¿quánto?**
how much?

30 /k/ **ecuivalente / equivalente**
equivalent

How to remember spelling rules:

Tip 1   If you find it hard to memorize these spelling rules in the abstract, learn a list of model words. For example, instead of trying to learn that **c** is hard before **a**, **o**, and **u**, just remember Cádiz, Colombia, Cuba or any other three that stick in your mind more easily: for example, **una casa en la costa cubana**. For **g**, remember **gata, gota, gusto** [cat, drop, taste], or choose your own. Sometimes they are easier to remember if you make your memory-help sentences silly (**¿el galés gordo me gusta?**), or if they relate to your own life somehow.

Tip 2   Acquire the habit of looking at the last sound of the stem of any verb that you are using and be ready to be on your guard against **c, g, gu, qu,** and **z**. Again, if letters are hard to remember, have a memorized list of sample verbs for yourself. For example, you could use **llegar** and **seguir** to remind yourself what to do with any other verb with a /g/ at the end of the stem; **cazar** and **vencer** are useful models for /Θ/; **tocar** is probably all you need for hard /k/ (regular **-er** and **-ir** verbs with that sound at the end of the stem are rare, but if you want one for the sake of completeness, there is **delinquir** [to break the law]). For /x/, follow **coger** when it is spelt with a **g** and if you want to remind yourself not to touch a verb with a **j** at the end of the stem, remember **bajar**.

Science is obviously a huge area. The exercises for today focus on relatively painless ways of expanding your vocabulary a little in the domain of science, using the techniques you know by now: linking unfamiliar words to more familiar cognates and encouraging you to practise guessing intelligently. The good news is that complicated technical words are very often the most easily 'guessable' once you have a feel for the ending and gender to go for.

la ciencia science, BUT ALSO knowledge

Guess the meaning:

> **1** el árbol de la ciencia del bien y del mal
>
> ....

el/la científico/-a scientist
la conciencia conscience, but also
   consciousness, awareness
concienzudo conscientious

físico physical
la física physics
el/la físico/-a physicist
el físico physique

> **2** Guess *metaphysical:* _ _ _ _ _ _ _ _ _ _
>
> **3** Guess *nuclear physics:* _ _ _ _ _ _ _ _ _ _ _ _ _ _ _

químico chemical   **la química** chemistry

> **4** Based on the relationship between **la física** and **el/la físico/-a**, guess how you say *a chemist:*
>
> **un/una** _ _ _ _ _ _ _ **/-a** (chemistry scholar, not a pharmacist).

| **el producto químico** chemical | **genético** genetic **la genética** genetics | **el gene** gene **el/la genetista** geneticist |

Guess the meaning:

> **5** Guess the meaning: **la ingeniería genética**
>
> ....

| **biológico** biological | **la biología** biology | **el/la biólogo/-a** biologist |

Based on the 'biology' pattern, try to generate equivalent trios of terms for theology, astrology, and anthropology:

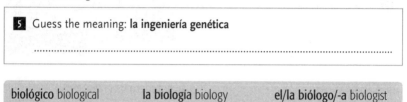

> **6** *theological*   **teo** _ _ _ _ _ _
>
>   *theology*   _ _   _ _ _ _ _ _ _ _
>
>   *theologian*   **el/la** _ _ _ _ _ _ _ **/ -a**
>
> **7** *astrological*   **astro** _ _ _ _ _ _
>
>   *astrology*   _ _   _ _ _ _ _ _ _ _ _
>
>   *astrologer*   **el/la** _ _ _ _ _ _ _ _ _ **/ -a**
>
> **8** *anthropological*   **antropo** _ _ _ _ _ _
>
>   *anthropology*   _ _   _ _ _ _ _ _ _ _ _ _ _
>
>   *anthropologist*   **el/la** _ _ _ _ _ _ _ _ _ _ _ **/ -a**

You could extend this list to cover archaeology (based on **arqueológico**), ethnology (based on **etnológico**), psychology (**psicológico**), and so on.

| **la experiencia** experience, BUT ALSO experiment **experimentar** to experience, and to experiment **experimentado** experienced **experimental** experimental **la experimentación** experimentation | **probar** to test, to prove, to try on (clothes), and to taste/test (food for flavour) **la prueba** trial, ALSO proof (NB a pointer to the fact that **probar** is radical-changing too.) **el probador** changing room **la probeta** test tube |

> **9** Guess the meaning of **el/la niño/-a probeta**:
>
> ....

la **contaminación** pollution

10	Guess *to pollute:*

_ _ _ _ _ _ _ _ _

el **invierno** winter   el **invernadero** greenhouse

11 Guess *greenhouse effect:* _ _   _ _ _ _ _ _ _
_ _ _ _ _ _ _ _ _ _

12 Guess *greenhouse gas:* _ _   _ _ _   _ _ _ _ _ _ _ _ _ _ _

avanzar (spelling changes needed) to advance
el avance advance

el progreso progress (as a general concept)
los progresos progress (in the sense of specific steps forward in particular field)

investigar sobre (spelling changes needed) to conduct research on, to investigate
la investigación research, piece of research, investigation
el/la investigador/-ora researcher, investigator

13 Guess *to progress:* _ _ _ _ _ _ _ _ _ _

el/la progre person with fashionably progressive political views, 'trendy lefty'

el proyecto plan, project
proyectar to project (i.e. throw)
el proyectil missile

el proyecto de ley bill (in the sense of planned law not yet approved by parliament)

Fill the gaps.

14 – 16   En la escuela, prefería _ _   _ _ _ _ _ _ _ a _ _
_ _ _ _ _ _ _, pero en cuanto a _ _   _ _ _ _ _ _ _ _ _,
no l _ aguantaba.
At school I preferred physics to chemistry, but as far as biology was concerned, I couldn't stand it.

17 Su hijo no es muy inteligente, pero es tan _ _ _ _ _ _ _ _ _ _ _
que suele sacar buenas notas en sus exámenes.
*Her son isn't very clever, but he is so conscientious that he usually gets quite
good exam results.*

18 – 19 Me preocupan mucho los problemas del medio ambiente, sobre todo lo
que nos dicen _ _ _ _ _ _ _ _ _ _ _ _ _ _ sobre _ _
_ _ _ _ _ _ _ _ _ _ _ _ _ _ _ _ _ .
*Environmental problems worry me a great deal, especially what the
scientists are telling us about the greenhouse effect.*

20 No creo en _ _ _ _ _ _ _ _ _ _ _ _ _ .
I don't believe in astrology.

21 En los últimos años han hecho grandes _ _ _ _ _ _ _ _ _ en
la terapia de los cancerosos.
*Great progress has been made in recent years in the treatment of cancer
patients.*

22 – 23 _ _ _ _ _ _ _ _ _ _ _ _ _ de _ _ _ _ _ _ _ _ _ _ _ _ _
científica son a veces muy costosos y por lo tanto es bastante difícil
conseguir la financiación necesaria.
*Scientific research projects are sometimes very costly and it is therefore quite
difficult to secure the necessary funding.*

24 – 25 _ _ _ _ _ _ _ _ _ _ _ _ _ _ _ _ no se limitan a
_ _ _ _ _ _ _ _ _ _ sobre los pueblos primitivos.
*Anthropologists do not limit themselves to researching into primitive
peoples.*

26 – 27 No basta con decir que es peligroso consumir _ _ _ _ _ _ _ _ _
_ _ _ _ _ _ _ _ en la comida; hay que _ _ _ _ _ _ lo.
*It is not enough to say that it is dangerous to consume chemicals in one's
food; it has to be proven.*

28 _ _ _ _ _ _ _ _ _ _ _ _ _ _ _ del Mar Mediterráneo es
una tragedia auténtica para los que nos acordamos de cómo era en los
años sesenta.
*The pollution of the Mediterranean is a real tragedy for those of us who
remember what it used to be like in the sixties.*

29 – 30 _ _ _ _ _ _ _ _ _ _ _ en _ _ _ _ _ _ _ _ dan miedo a
algunos, que hablan de _ _ _ _ _ _ _ _ _ _ _ _ _ _ _ _ _ al
estilo de Frankenstein.
*Advances in genetics frighten some people, who talk about Frankenstein-
type experimentation.*

Optional extras

Is there a branch of science which interests you in particular? If there is, make sure you have looked up and learnt the specialized vocabulary you would need to talk or write about it. See how much of it you can guess before you start looking up and you might be pleasantly surprised.

Students often complain that imperatives in Spanish are terribly muddling, but it usually turns out that students are muddled by their flawed command of the verb conjugations combined with a sense of panic that overcomes them when they try to decide what they are aiming at. Rock-solid verbs and a cool head are all it takes to get imperatives right every time; there is nothing difficult to understand and no subtle decisions have to be made.

I   What is an imperative?

Some Spanish teachers use the term 'command', which is sometimes helpful, but it can also be misleading as we often use the imperative when we are being polite or casual, and not issuing commands at all. For example, 'Don't ask me why', 'Have a biscuit', and 'Come off it!' are all phrases that use the English imperative.

II   Present subjunctive to form imperatives

There are various forms for the imperative because

▶ there are four words for 'you' in Spanish: **tú** and **vosotros**; **usted** and **ustedes**;

▶ the familiar forms are different in the affirmative and negative.

But only two of them – the familiar affirmatives – are uniquely used as imperatives. All the rest – i.e. the familiar negative, and all of the polite forms – are, in fact, simply the present subjunctive.

Translate the following using the present subjunctive:

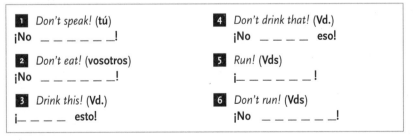

1 *Don't speak!* (**tú**)
¡No _ _ _ _ _ _!

2 *Don't eat!* (**vosotros**)
¡No _ _ _ _ _ _!

3 *Drink this!* (**Vd.**)
¡_ _ _ _ esto!

4 *Don't drink that!* (**Vd.**)
¡No _ _ _ _ eso!

5 *Run!* (**Vds**)
¡_ _ _ _ _ _!

6 *Don't run!* (**Vds**)
¡No _ _ _ _ _ _!

III Familiar affirmative forms of regular verbs

These are as follows:

-ar verbs, e.g. **hablar**:	habla	hablad
-er verbs, e.g. **comer**:	come	comed
-ir verbs, e.g. **vivir**:	vive	vivid

It helps some students to note that the **tú** form is the present indicative with the **s** dropped, as that matches the French form.

Radical-changing verbs behave predictably in these forms: the **-ar** and **-er** verbs, called the 'first pattern' in this book, continue to follow the rule that the change is only made when the stress falls on the stem. That means that the change occurs in the **tú** form, but not in the **vosotros** form. For example:

entender:	entiende	entended

The second and third patterns are not anomalous in these forms. For example:

mentir:	miente	mentid
pedir:	pide	pedid

IV Irregular familiar affirmative forms

Irregular verbs often have an irregular, monsyllabic **tú** form that has to be memorized, but are regular in the **vosotros** form. For example:

salir:	sal	salid
venir:	ven	venid

The irregular **tú** imperatives are not listed here, since they can be found in any good dictionary or verb list. Make sure you have revised them, and once you think you know them, try the following spot check.

Make the negative imperatives affirmative. They are all in the **tú** form.

---

7 No me digas cómo acaba la película.

_ _ _ _ _ cómo acaba la película.
Tell me how the film ends.

8 No me hagas caso.

_ _ _ _ _ caso.
Mark my words.

9 No te pongas ese sombrero.

_ _ _ _ _ ese sombrero.
Put that hat on.

10 No vengas a verme esta tarde.

_ _ _ a verme esta tarde.
Come and see me this afternoon.

11 No seas malo.

_ _ bueno.
Be good.

Follow the flow diagram and you will always be right:

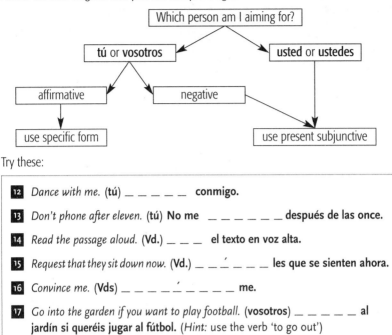

Try these:

> **12** *Dance with me.* (**tú**) _ _ _ _ _ **conmigo.**
>
> **13** *Don't phone after eleven.* (**tú**) **No me** _ _ _ _ _ _ **después de las once.**
>
> **14** *Read the passage aloud.* (**Vd.**) _ _ _ **el texto en voz alta.**
>
> **15** *Request that they sit down now.* (**Vd.**) _ _ _́ _ _ _ **les que se sienten ahora.**
>
> **16** *Convince me.* (**Vds**) _ _ _ _ _́ _ _ _ _ **me.**
>
> **17** *Go into the garden if you want to play football.* (**vosotros**) _ _ _ _ _ **al jardín si queréis jugar al fútbol.** (*Hint:* use the verb 'to go out')

V Pronouns

As questions 7, 8 and 9 above should have reminded you, pronouns become suffixes in all of the affirmative imperatives, but remain in their normal position, preceding the verb in negative imperatives. For example:

¡Háblame! [Speak to me!] (**tú**)
¡No me hables! [Don't speak to me!] (**tú**)

Think carefully about accents here: appending a pronoun as a suffix adds a syllable to the verb form, so you must re-think whether an accent is needed when you do this. Go back to your stress rules if you need to, and revise them before attempting the next exercise.

Put an accent on the imperatives which require one.

> **18** **Buscalo en el comedor.**
> *Look for it in the dining-room.*
>
> **19** **Decidles que no lo hagan.**
> *Tell them not to do it.*
>
> **20**
>
>
> *Please buy me it*

The affirmative **vosotros** form drops its final **d** before the reflexive pronoun, **os**. So, for example, 'Sit down', in the **vosotros** form is: **Sentaos** (**sentad + os**). There is one exception and that is **Idos** for 'Go away'. However, many Spanish speakers prefer to use the infinitive and so would say **Sentaros** for 'Sit down', but this is not recommended and Spaniards who say it themselves will sometimes 'correct' foreigners who use it!

To make imperatives negative means:

▶ switching to the present subjunctive for the **tú** and **vosotros** forms;

▶ staying with the present subjunctive for the **usted** and **ustedes** forms;

▶ moving any pronouns back to their usual position before the verb; and

▶ checking accents if the number of syllables in the word changes.

Ring the right person and make the following imperatives negative.

---

21 **Dame un beso.**   tú/vosotros
_ _ _ _ _ _ _ un beso.   usted/ustedes
Don't give me a kiss.

22 **Venid a cenar mañana.**   tú/vosotros
_ _ _ _ _ _ _ _ _ _ a cenar mañana.   usted/ustedes
Don't come for dinner tomorrow.

23 **Levántense por favor.**   tú/vosotros
_ _ _ _ _ _ _ _ _ _ _ _ por favor.   usted/ustedes
Don't get up, please.

24 **Acostaos en seguida.**   tú/vosotros
_ _ _ _ _ _ _ _ _ _ _ _ en seguida.   usted/ustedes
Don't go to bed straight away.

25 **Haga seguir mi correo a mi nueva dirección.**   tú/vosotros
_ _ _ _ _ _ seguir mi correo a mi nueva dirección.   usted/ustedes
Don't forward my post to my new address.

26 **¡Idos ahora mismo!**   tú/vosotros
¡_ _ _ _ _ _ _ _ _ _ ahora mismo!   usted/ustedes
Don't go right now!

VI Nosotros forms

There is an additional form of the imperative for the first-person plural. In English its equivalent is 'let's + verb', for example, 'let's dance'. There are two choices in Spanish. You can either use **vamos a** + infinitive, (for example, **vamos a bailar**), or you can use the present subjunctive of the verb (for example, **bailemos**). In the affirmative, the **vamos a** + infinitive is more common nowadays and easier to use, so why not stick to that? In the negative, the present subjunctive is a better choice.

Ir is the only irregular verb in this form: instead of having **¡Vayamos!**, it has **¡Vamos!** for 'Let's go'. It is also often found in the reflexive form of **¡Vámonos!**

Note how the final **s** of **vamos** is dropped before adding the **-nos** suffix. This is true of all reflexive verbs in the **nosotros** form of the imperative if you decide to use the present subjunctive option, but as it is a further complicating factor, you may consider it all the more reason to stick to the **vamos a** + infinitive formula.

Try these:

---

27 *Let's have lunch now.* _ _ _ _ _ _ _ _ _ _ _ **ahora.**

28 *Let's not have lunch before they get here.*
   No _ _ _ _ _ _ _ **antes de que lleguen.**

29 *Let's wait for them.* _ _ _ _ _ _ _ _ _ _ _ _ **les.**

30 *Let's not wait for them.* **No les** _ _ _ _ _ _ _ _ _ **.**

All types of writing (and speech) can be greatly enriched by the judicious integration of set expressions, similes, and metaphors. You probably use more than you realize in English and you can enliven your Spanish if you start to make an active effort on this front. It will also help you understand the language better, since some are 'unguessable', even if you know the meaning of the individual words that make up an expression.

For example, the saying **en todas partes cuecen habas** is quite opaque, even if you know that it literally means 'everywhere they cook broad beans'! (In fact, it is used to comment philosophically on something negative which is to be found everywhere; it might be a rejoinder to someone's complaint about graffiti in Madrid, to point out that it is not only Madrid that has the problem).

This example also illustrates another point: some set expressions have no equivalent in English; others have only approximate translations, while a few have identical versions, often because they are derived from a source common to both cultures, such as the Bible. For example, **lavarse las manos de un problema**, 'to wash one's hands of a problem', exists in both languages because its common origin is Pontius Pilate in the New Testament.

A bonus outcome of learning set expressions and figures of speech is to be had when you did not know beforehand all the words contained in one; it also helps you to remember individual words. For example, having learnt **en todas partes cuecen habas**, the verb **cocer** and its radical-changing behaviour, as well as the word for 'broad beans', **habas**, might be remembered more easily. If you are one of those persistent offenders who keep forgetting that **mano** is feminine, remembering the phrase **lavarse las manos de . . .** might just fix it in your memory once and for all.

For these reasons, the literal meaning will be given in parentheses for all of the expressions in today's lists. Make sure you learn not only what the expression as a whole means, but also any of its component parts that you did not already know.

I Similes

Similes are in widespread use and not always obvious because the defining adjective is often omitted. Some examples are:

Me puse como un tomate I turned as red as a lobster (literally, a tomato)
Está como una cabra S/he is as mad as a hatter (literally, a goat)
Era (fuerte) como un toro He was as strong as an ox (literally, a bull)
Estaba como boca de lobo It was pitch-dark (literally, like the mouth of a wolf)

una mentira como una casa a whopper of a lie (literally, like a house.)
como un pulpo en un garaje like a fish out of water, at sea (literally, like an octopus in a garage)

Check you have learnt these by giving the image for the adjective:

1 oscuro *dark*
como _ _ _ _   _ _
_ _ _ _

2 fuerte *strong*
como _ _   _ _ _ _

3 despistado *lost*
como _ _   _ _ _ _ _
_ _   _ _   _ _ _ _ _ _

4 grande *big*
como _ _ _   _ _ _ _

5 rojo *red*
como _ _   _ _ _ _ _ _

6 loco *mad*
como _ _ _   _ _ _ _ _

Where the defining adjective is included, one finds **más** + adjective + **que** . . . at least as often as tan + adjective + **como** . . . . Thus, **más rojo que un tomate** would be at least as commonly used, if not more so, than **tan rojo como un tomate**, because in the latter case it would tend to be shortened, as we have seen, to **como un tomate**.

II Words of wisdom
The following sayings, or proverbs, are well worth learning.

En boca
cerrada no
entran
moscas

en boca cerrada no entran moscas
keep your mouth shut and you'll stay out of trouble (literally, 'flies do not enter a closed mouth')
no hay mal que por bien no venga
every cloud has a silver lining (literally, 'there is no evil which does not come for the sake of good')
querer es poder where there's a will there's a way (literally, 'to want is to be able')

no es oro todo lo que reluce all that glitters is not gold
a quien madruga Dios le ayuda the early bird catches the worm (literally, 'God helps s/he who rises early')
hay gustos que merecen palos there's no accounting for tastes (literally, 'there are tastes that deserve sticks', i.e. a beating)
el ocio es madre de todos los vicios the devil makes work for idle hands (literally, 'idleness is the mother of all vices')
quien siembra vientos recoge tempestades literally, s/he who sows winds, reaps storms, i.e. if you make trouble on a small scale, you will get it back on a much bigger one – a little like the idea of 'chickens coming home to roost' in English

When you think you have learnt these, draw lines to pair up the beginnings with the ends of the expressions.

7 hay gustos ...	... recoge tempestades
8 querer ...	... todo lo que reluce
9 quien siembra vientos ...	... es poder
10 el ocio es ...	... no entran moscas
11 no hay mal ...	... que merecen palos
12 a quien madruga ...	... madre de todos los vicios
13 no es oro ...	... que por bien no venga
14 en boca cerrada ...	... Dios le ayuda

III Figures of speech

Learn these figures of speech.

mentar la soga en casa del ahorcado literally, 'to mention the rope in the house of the hanged man' – i.e. 'to touch a raw nerve by speaking tactlessly'

estar en el séptimo cielo to be in seventh heaven

ser más católico que el Papa to go too far, to be more zealous than necessary (literally, 'to be more Catholic than the Pope')

con el alma en un hilo with one's heart in one's mouth (literally, with one's soul on a thread)

coger el toro por los cuernos to take the bull by the horns

perder los estribos to lose one's temper (literally, one's stirrups)

a lo hecho, pecho it's no use crying over spilt milk (literally, 'to what is done, chest', i.e. face it)

en carne y hueso in the flesh (in flesh and bone)

de carne y hueso real, live, human, flesh-and-blood (of flesh and bone)

con viento en popa literally, with the wind behind you – a tailwind; in other words; a wind helping you go in the direction you want – used when something is going well, or making great progress (**la popa** the stern of a ship, cf. poop deck)

no tener ni voz ni voto to have no say at all (literally, 'to have neither voice nor vote')

poner el dedo en la llaga to put your finger on it (when 'it' is something sensitive or negative) (literally, 'to put one's finger on the open sore'); if positive choose **dar en el clavo**

coger a alguien con las manos en la masa to catch s.one red-handed (literally, with his/her hands in the dough)

pedir peras al olmo to ask the impossible (literally, 'to ask pears of an elm tree')

de uvas a peras once in a blue moon (literally, 'from grapes to pears')

Can you reproduce from memory the two sayings that are exactly like English?

---

15 *to be in seventh heaven:* **estar en el**
_ _ _ _ _ _ _
_ _ _ _ _

16 *to take the bull by the horns:* **coger**
_ _ _ _ _ _ _ _ _
_ _ _ _ _ _ _ _ _ _

And from this section's introductory comments:

---

17 *to wash one's hands of:*   _ _ _ _ _ _ _ _ _ _ _ _ _ _ _ _ _

Try to finish the following expressions and provide a translation. Score a point for every one that you can complete and translate without looking back. When you have done all you can like that, copy the translations from above and then try to fill in the Spanish without looking back. Score a half point for any you complete in this way.

---

18 **mentar la soga** _ _ _ _ _ _
_ _ _ _ _ _ _ _ _ _
....

19 **coger a alguien con las manos**
_ _ _ _ _ _ _ _
....

20 **poner el dedo** _ _ _ _
_ _ _ _
....

21 **con viento** _ _ _ _ _ _
....

22 **ser más católico** _ _ _ _ _
_ _ _ _
....

23 **pedir peras** _ _ _ _ _ _
....

24 **no tener ni voz** _ _ _ _ _ _
....

25 **a lo hecho,** _ _ _ _ _
....

26 **perder** _ _ _ _ _ _ _ _ _ _
....

27 **de carne** _ _ _ _ _ _
....

28 **de uvas** _ _ _ _ _ _
....

29 **con el alma** _ _ _ _
_ _ _ _
....

30 **en carne** _ _ _ _ _ _
....

If you find these set expressions amusing, why not collect more? When you are looking up an individual word you will often see set expressions that include it listed in the dictionary entry. Note down those you particularly like and it will help you to memorize the word you were looking up in the first place. What is more, it will upgrade the quality of your Spanish.

Medley of minor points

The end of this revision programme is approaching and you should be feeling much more confident by now. Today is devoted to a medley of small points that you can easily clear up even at this late stage. So you will have saved yourself a few extra marks, as well as reinforced the impression of accuracy and precision that you want to give not only to your examiners, but anyone else with whom you communicate in Spanish.

I   y and e [and]

Don't forget to change **y** to **e** whenever it is followed by a word starting with an /i/ sound. Remember that it is the sound that counts, not the spelling, so the word might be spelt '**hi-**' or '**i-**'. However, not all words that start with these letters will demand the change. For example, **el hielo** [ice] is pronounced 'yelo', so you would say **fuego y hielo** [fire and ice]. Contrast this with **el hilo** [thread], where you would have to change the **y** to **e**: **tela e hilo** [fabric and thread]. Stress is not an issue with this rule: no matter where the stress falls on the word starting with the /i/ sound, you must change **y** to **e**. Here is an example of a case where the stress is nowhere near the /i/, but the change still has to be made: **Fernando e Isabel**. Memorize it to remind yourself that stress is immaterial to this rule.

II   o and u [or]

An analogous rule exists for **o**. Change **o** to **u** before a word starting with an /o/ sound. For example: **diez u once** [ten or eleven]. As before, stress is irrelevant: **casas u hoteles** [houses or hotels].

III   ó [or]   ·

An accent is added to **o** when it appears between numbers written in figures, to avoid confusion with a zero: **20 ó 30** [20 or 30].

Now, read the following as if you were checking your own work. Tick any that are correct and rectify any mistakes with **y, e, o, u**, and **ó**.

> **1** La relación entre padre y hijo es muy importante.
> *The father–son relationship is a very important one.*
>
> **2** El artículo es lúcido e interesante.
> *The article is lucid and interesting.*
>
> **3** Quince ó veinte personas asistieron a la conferencia.
> *Fifteen or twenty people attended the lecture.*

4 No sé si la cita **es** de Virgilio o Homero.
I don't know if the quotation is from Virgil or Homer.

5 Somos unos 25 o 26 alumnos en mi clase.
There are about 25 or 26 pupils in my class.

6 Es un producto químico que mata musgos y hierba.
It is a chemical that kills mosses and grass.

7 Es un libro de gramática inglesa concebido para francófonos y hispanoparlantes.
It is an English grammar book designed for French and Spanish speakers.

IV el and un before feminine nouns

The article **la** becomes **el** and **una** becomes **un** before a feminine noun beginning with a stressed /a/ sound: you must say **el agua** [water], but **la amapola** [poppy]. Since it is sound which is the decisive factor here again, '**ha-**' demands the change just as much as '**a-**'. For example, **el hacha** [axe] is feminine. Note that the noun remains feminine despite the use of the masculine article, so any adjectives will still have the feminine agreement. For example: **el agua fría** [cold water]; **un hada madrina** [a fairy godmother]. And again, since avoidance of the /a/ from the article running into the /a/ at the beginning of the word is the point of this rule, if something like an adjective happens to separate the article from the noun, the change will not be necessary: **la poca agua potable que queda** [the little drinking water left].

A common mistake

Students often confuse this rule with patterns of unpredictable genders, thinking, for example, that the fact that you have to say **el agua** makes it masculine. Make it clear to yourself in your notes that this is not the case. List words like **agua**, **alma** [soul], **hada**, **águila** [eagle] with an annotation as a reminder such as '**el** – (fem.)'.
Note these have nothing to do with words like **sistema** [system] which are masculine even though they end in 'a'.

Ring the correct gender and article for each of the following. Score a whole point if you get the gender and the article right, but a half point if you only get one of the two right.

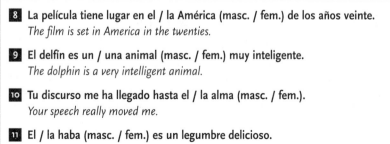

8 La película tiene lugar en el / la América (masc. / fem.) de los años veinte.
The film is set in America in the twenties.

9 El delfín es un / una animal (masc. / fem.) muy inteligente.
The dolphin is a very intelligent animal.

10 Tu discurso me ha llegado hasta el / la alma (masc. / fem.).
Your speech really moved me.

11 El / la haba (masc. / fem.) es un legumbre delicioso.
The broad bean is a delicious vegetable.

12 La vida de un / una ama de casa
(masc. / fem.) puede ser frustrante.
Housewives' lives can be frustrating.

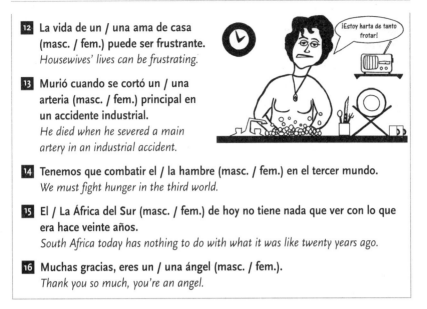

13 Murió cuando se cortó un / una
arteria (masc. / fem.) principal en
un accidente industrial.
*He died when he severed a main
artery in an industrial accident.*

14 Tenemos que combatir el / la hambre (masc. / fem.) en el tercer mundo.
We must fight hunger in the third world.

15 El / La África del Sur (masc. / fem.) de hoy no tiene nada que ver con lo que
era hace veinte años.
South Africa today has nothing to do with what it was like twenty years ago.

16 Muchas gracias, eres un / una ángel (masc. / fem.).
Thank you so much, you're an angel.

V   Adverbs

You already know that Spanish uses adverbs less than English. But that does not mean it
<u>never</u> does, so you should know how to form an adverb correctly from an adjective for
those occasions when its use is the most appropriate choice to make. This is all the more
important since it is so easy and it would be a crime to allow yourself to lose a mark for it!
You simply take the feminine of an adjective and add **-mente**. For example, to make an
adverb out of **afortunado** [lucky], first make it feminine: **afortunada**; then add **-mente**:
afortunadamente [luckily, fortunately].

If the feminine is the same as the masculine, there is even less to do. For example, to
make an adverb out of **enorme** [enormous], the feminine is also **enorme**, so just add
-mente to that: **enormemente** [enormously].

Make adverbs from the following adjectives:

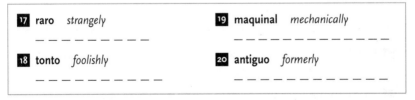

17 raro   *strangely*

— — — — — — — —

18 tonto   *foolishly*

— — — — — — — —

19 maquinal   *mechanically*

— — — — — — — — — — —

20 antiguo   *formerly*

— — — — — — — — — —

One possible catch that was mentioned on Day 8 is that if an adjective has an accent, it
keeps it when it becomes an adverb even though there is now a new stress on the first 'e'
of **-mente**. For example, **rápido** [quick] becomes **rápidamente**.

Try these:

---

21   **fácil**   *easy*   **22**   **increíble**   *incredible*

— — — — — — — —   — — — — — — — — — —

Has this made you realize you are still shaky on how to make adjectives feminine? If so, look back to Day 1 in this book and if that is not enough, go back to your reference grammar and go through agreements once more. This is a good illustration of how language skills build on each other: you cannot ignore feeble or non-existent foundations, so do not hesitate to devote as long as it takes to reinforce them.

The final point to remember about adverbs is that if you want to use two or more together, only the last has the **-mente** while those which come before are left in the intermediate phase of the feminine form but without **-mente**. For example:

> **Estaba agotado física y mentalmente**. [He was mentally and physically exhausted.]

Note the feminine ending of **física** even though the sentence is referring to a man. This is because it is not an adjective but an adverb without the **-mente** tagged on.

Try these:

---

23   **Estaba en el séptimo cielo: era**   _ _ _ _ _   **y**
      _ _ _ _ _ _ _ _ _   **feliz.**
      He was in seventh heaven: stupidly, madly happy.

24   **Estaba**   _ _ _ _ _,   _ _ _ _ _ _ _ _ _ _ , **y**
      _ _ _ _ _ _ _ _ _ _ _ _ _   **furioso.**
      He was blindly, violently, savagely angry.

As these sentences indicate, such successions of adverbs give quite a dramatic – sometimes verging on the melodramatic – feel to your style. So make sure that is what you intend if you decide to use them.

However, pleased as you may be that you can form adverbs correctly, remember that you should still try to find an alternative first:

> either simply an adjective:
> **Le habló enfadado**   [He spoke to her angrily]

> or an abstract noun:
> **La miró con amor**   [He looked at her lovingly]
> **Se lo explicó con paciencia**   [He patiently explained]

> or by turning the sentence around:
> **Le echó una mirada de amor**   [He looked at her lovingly]

> or by using **manera**, or **modo**:
> **Se lo dijo de modo brusco**   [He said it abruptly]

VI Diminutives and augmentatives

Although rules are to be found on how to form these, creating your own diminutive and augmentative endings is a risky business as there are just too many anomalous ones for rules to be reliable. A safer bet is to listen and look out for the ones used by native speakers and try to use those yourself. It is worth doing as it will definitely make your Spanish less foreign-sounding. *Remember* that augmentatives and diminutives do not only reveal something of what you are talking about, but also about your attitude to your subject, and your frame of mind at the time of speaking. If you say **tengo que perder tres kilitos**, you are minimizing or making light of the effort involved to lose the three kilos: obviously, the kilos themselves are invariable. Here are just six examples, to start your collection:

la casita (sweet) little house	**una horita, media horita** just an hour, a quick half-hour	in a gentle way as to a small child: 'dame un besito'
la casucha ugly/poky little house/hovel	**un besito** a little kiss, or a normal kiss, but spoken	**una risilla** irritating little laugh, giggle
la carita little face		

Fill the gaps and provide a translation:

25 Dame media _ _ _ _ _ _ y estoy de vuelta.

....

26 Viven en una _ _ _ _ _ _ _ _ sin jardín, en un barrio bajo de la ciudad.

....

27 Al ver su _ _ _ _ _ _ sonriéndome, me sentí mejor en seguida.

....

28 Hemos comprado una _ _ _ _ _ _ en la costa.

....

29 Dale un _ _ _ _ _ _ a tu muñeca antes de acostarla.

....

30 La muy tonta soltó una _ _ _ _ _ _ _ porque no quería parecer pudibunda.

....

Vocabulary:
Bumper self-test

DAY
29

How effective are your vocabulary-learning strategies? This book should have helped you develop and improve them. But today you can find out how much you have really assimilated. See how you score, without looking back in the first instance. This will be the result to record on your Progress Chart (see page 164), but then put the gaps that you left and the mistakes that you made to good purpose by going back and completing the test with help. As you write in the answers that you missed, try saying them out loud at the same time, just in case you have a better aural than visual memory.

Behind the scenes

The vocabulary for today is just a spot-check of all that has been covered, but if you manage to score above 20 points out of 30, that probably means you have increased your vocabulary by more than two-thirds of what is in this book, since the easiest words are not the ones selected for the exercise. If you achieve fewer than 15 points out of 30, you have not yet found the best strategy for the way your own memory works: ask yourself what you find easy to remember and analyse why. For example, if it is song lyrics you might be someone who needs to learn vocabulary out loud and group words rhythmically so that you can almost chant them to yourself. Some people can memorize best from their own handwriting, in which case staring at a printed page is a mistake: copy everything out and the copying itself might be enough to fix it.

Treat yourself to a new pen to make it an attractive prospect! Try using yellow paper: some claim it is easier on the eyes. Others get nowhere looking at their own handwriting and need to type everything out with wide line spacing. Whichever is your own best method – and the sooner you work that out, the quicker and better you will be able to revise in the future – only the very fortunate few can learn effectively by just reading through printed lists.

1	*straight hair*	_ _ _ _ _ _ _ _ _ _
2	*to face up to, confront*	_ _ _ _ _ _ _ _ _ _ _ _
3	*miserly*	_ _ _ _ _ _
4	*governmental*	_ _ _ _ _ _ _ _ _ _ _ _

5 democrat   el/la _ _ _ _ _ _ _ _

6 easy-going   _ _ _ _ _ _ _ _ _ _

7 art gallery   _ _ _ _ _ _ _ _ _

8 to sketch   _ _ _ _ _ _ _

9 crimson   _ _ _ _ _ _ _

10 syllable   _ _ _ _ _ _ _

11 offstage, behind the scenes   _ _ _ _ _
                                        _ _ _ _ _ _ _ _ _

12 foothills   _ _ _
                                        _ _ _ _ _ _ _ _ _ _ _

13 Algerian   _ _ _ _ _ _ _

14 without beating about the bush   _ _ _ _ _ _ _ _ _

15 empire   _ _ _ _ _ _ _ _

16 relentless   sin _ _ _ _ _ _

17 out of tune   _ _ _ _ _ _ _ _

18 tambourine   _ _ _ _ _ _ _ _ _ _

19 screenplay   _ _ _ _ _ _ _

20 news headlines   _ _ _ _ _ _ _ _ _ _

21 truancy   _ _ _ _ _ _ _ _ _ _

22 academic year   _ _ _ _ _ _ _

23 carcinogenic   _ _ _ _ _ _ _ _ _ _ _

24 Spanish NHS   _ _ _ _ _ _ _ _ _ _ _
                                        _ _ _ _ _ _

25 to shriek   _ _ _ _ _ _ _

26 to grumble   _ _ _ _ _ _ _ _ _

27 biologist   el/la _ _ _ _ _ _ _ /-a

28 greenhouse   _ _ _ _ _ _ _ _ _ _ _

29 to lose one's temper   _ _ _ _ _ _ _ _ _
                                        _ _ _ _ _ _ _

30 pitch-dark   como _ _ _ _ _ _
                                        _ _ _ _

Ask yourself these questions:

▶ Are you confident that from now on you can avoid making elementary mistakes of the kinds covered in *Upgrade?*

▶ Have you sorted out the minor points that you had never really got clear in your own mind?

▶ Finally, have you trained your eye to spot slips of the pen?

See how successful you have been by studying the 30 sentences below. Each one may have any number of mistakes, or may be completely correct. Tick the correct sentences and put right any mistakes you see.

Check your answers against the answer section. For the scoring, you get one mark for every sentence you recognize rightly as correct and for any in which you are able to put right all the errors. For sentences where you are right in part but not in full, give yourself a half mark.

To practise your checking method for examination purposes, do not try to spot errors in each sentence one by one: read through all the sentences for one type of mistake at a time. For example:

i) first look for questions and exclamations with missing accents in all the sentences;

ii) then look for missing or incorrect agreements;

iii) next look at the verb forms. *Remember* you cannot check a verb unless you know:

▶ its infinitive;
▶ whether it is regular, irregular, or radical-changing – if so, which type;
▶ what tense, mood, and person it is meant to be in.

iv) now look at the accents for distinguishing purposes; then accents for stress; and then **y/e** and **o/u/ó**;

v) finally look at punctuation and capitalization.

Only then will you be able to see which you can tick as quite correct.

---

1 Susana es demasiada joven para acompañarnos.

2 ¿A quien habrías votado en las elecciones generales, si habías podido?

3 Cuántas fotos te queden? ¿Me dejas sacar uno?

4 Paris me encanta como ciudad, pero me gustan menos los parisinos.

5 El surrealismo estaba un movimiento literario importante.

6 Lo que se vende como jamon de Parma en Inglaterra se parece al jamon serrano Español.

7 Atravesaba la meseta castellano desde hace dos días cuando vió la aldea que buscaba.

8 Quedaba al noroeste del camino que seguía.

9 Era donde había nacido y no lo veía desde hacia veintidos años.

10 Para mi, la censura es una tontería absurdo, en terminos generales, aunque claro que hay excepciones importantes.

11 Si hubiéramos estudiado temas modernos como el medio ambiente y la Segunda Guerra Mundial en las clases de geografía y historia, creo que me habrían gustado mucho mas.

12 Los sociólogos opinan que hay una relacion entre la pobreza y la delinquencia juvenil.

13 Estaba leyendo tranquilamente en la biblioteca cuando sentió un mano en el hombro.

14 El acento galés es más cantarín que el escoces.

15 No sé si podré ayudarte; todo dependeré en cuándo me necesitas.

16 De habermelo pedido antes, habrías podido contar conmigo.

17 Andó tres horas antes de encontrar quien le ayudara.

18 Te arrepentirás de esta locura, verás.

19 Dijó que si, que yo tenía razón, pero no hizo nada.

20 Su idea consistía de escaparse de Europa para ir a vivir a Africa ecuatorial.

Te arrepentirás de esta locura. Los tatuajes no son elegantes, cariño

21 Le toqué el brazo en señal de despedida.

22 ¿Dónde se coge el autobús para el centro? ¿Aqui mismo lo cojo? Gracias.

23 Para mí, usted tiene razón, pero mi marido tiene sus dudas; convénceselo como me ha convencido a mí y no habrá problema.

24 De los 80 o 90 personas que respondieron a nuestro cuestionario, aproximadamente tres cuartos prefirieron el güisqui escocés al irlandés.

25 La ingeniería genético es un gran avance científico pero las implicaciones éticas son difíciles y importantes.

26 Pídaselo a tu padre; yo no tengo tiempo.

27 No se lo dices, por favor, es un secreto.

28 Cuando sabí la verdad, no pude creermelo.

29 En cambio, cuando se lo explicé a Dolores, no se sorprendió en absoluto.

30 A diferencia de mí – y de ti, dicho sea de paso – a Dolores no le sorprende nada.

Progress Chart

Use this chart to track your daily progress. Use three colours: one for the vocabulary sections, one for grammar, and one for style. That way you will be able to see at a glance if you are weaker in one of the three areas and then make a special effort to compensate for that.

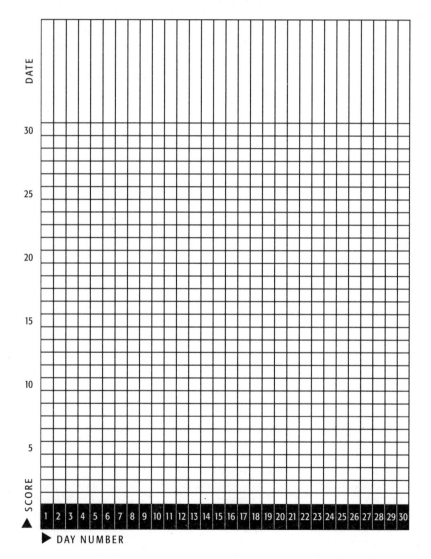

Answer to Exercises

Day 1 AGREEMENTS
1 tonta
2 comilona
3 fría
4 parlanchina
5 trabajadoras
6 importantes
7 fáciles
8–13 Al volver a la Universidad después de una estancia de tres años en Puerto Rico, Pedro Salinas escribió <u>algunos</u> (8) ensayos de crítica <u>literaria</u> (9) y puso el toque final [correct] a <u>algunas</u> (10) piezas teatrales [correct], pero sobre todo, en los últimos [correct] años de su vida, se concentró en la prosa <u>narrativa</u> (11). Publicó su relato orwelliano [correct], *La bomba impecable* [correct], y luchó con aquella [correct] novela que tanto [correct] trabajo le costaba, <u>titulada</u> (12) provisionalmente *El valor de la vida*, novela sobre el tema de la guerra que, por fin, dejó <u>inacabada</u> (13)
14–16 La ensalada había sido preparada con muchos ingredientes exóticos. [sido does not agree because it is part of a compound tense with haber].
17 ... tienen que haber terminado ...
18–19 Tengo leídas cien páginas, pero Cecilia ha leído la novela entera ya. [leídas agrees because it is with tener, not haber]
20 Correct
21–22 La tienda se estaba <u>cerrando</u> cuando llegó corriendo ... [present participles never agree]
23 La casa fue <u>destrozada</u> por el incendio
24–25 La abuela tiene <u>guardados</u> <u>muchos</u> recuerdos de su juventud
26–27 Las nietas no habían visto nunca tantas cosas <u>bonitas</u> [one mark for correcting bonitas, one mark for not correcting anything else!]
28 Estoy demasiado cansada ...
29 ... demasiada sal ... [adjectival use, so must agree]
30 No bebas demasiado ...

Day 2
DESCRIBING PEOPLE
1–2 high forehead – frente – and cropped hair – <u>despejada</u>
3 long, straight hair – pelo <u>liso</u> y <u>largo</u>
4–5 bearded and frowning
6–7 looking tired, with rings under his eyes
8 open-mouthed – <u>boquiabierta</u>, noticia <u>sorprendente</u>
9–10 large nose and raised eyebrows
11 neither with curly hair – pelo <u>rizado</u>
12 for getting all the underlined agreements right

13–21 Check against list provided in section

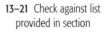

22 The missing word is un sinvergüenza
23 ... que se abrochen los cinturones de seguridad
24 ... dos camisetas nuevas ...
25–26 Llevaba tejanos [*or* vaqueros] y una gorra de visera
27 Abrígate ...
28 El traje de novia ... magnífico
29 ... que los niños anden descalzos ...
30 El público zapateó ...

Day 3
EASY CONSTRUCTIONS: SUBJUNCTIVE
1 Hagas lo que hagas ...
2 Ojalá me hubiera hecho caso ...
3 Quizá la vuelva a ver ...
4 Por poco probable que pueda parecer ...
5 Tenía el pelo tan desmelenado, era como si llevara semanas sin peinarse
6 Ojalá no se descubra nunca ...

7 dicho sea de paso

8 S

9 I

10 S

11 I

12 I

13 I

14 I

15 S

16 S

17 Por sorprendente que <u>pueda</u> parecer . . .

18 Diga lo que <u>diga</u> . . .

19 Correct

20 Correct

21 . . . de muy <u>buena</u> índole.

22 Por muy <u>guapos</u> que sean . . .

23 Ojalá se me <u>hubiera</u> ocurrido a tiempo

24 . . . como si fuera . . .

25 Vayas donde vayas

26 Ojalá encontremos la oportunidad . . .

27 Por absurdo que te pueda parecer . . .

28 . . . dicho sea de paso . . .

29 Quizá sea . . .

30 Ojalá me lo hubieras explicado . . .

Day 4
ACCENTS: NON-STRESS

1 ¿Dónde compraste esa camiseta tan original?

2 ¿Qué le dijiste para suavizar un poco la mala noticia?

3–4 No recuerdo dónde ni cuándo [or vice versa] la conocí

5 ¡Qué horror!

6 ¡Cuánta gente mal educada por aquí

7–8 ¿Por <u>qué</u> me tratas así? ¿Es porque no me quieres ya? – 'Is it because . . . ?' is a closed question, so no interrogative to put an accent on

9–12 ¿<u>Cuántas</u> veces tendré que repetirte que eso no tiene nada que ver?

13 No sé <u>cómo</u> te atreves a emplear este tono agresivo conmigo – indirect question

14–15 ¿Así que el fontanero no llegó hasta las seis? ¡Qué pesadilla! – closed question, followed by exclamation

16–17 ¿Recuerdas <u>cuánto</u> nos gustaba pasearnos por estas calles tan tranquilas cuando vivíamos aquí? – closed question containing exclamation

18 ¿Te das cuenta de la hora que es? – closed question

19 ¿Te das cuenta de <u>qué</u> hora es? – closed question containing indirect question

20 Explícame por <u>qué</u> has actuado así – indirect question

21–22 ¿<u>Cuál</u> de los ejercicios que [no accent] has hecho te costó más?

23–24 No te imaginas cuánto [correct] tiempo he pasado en esto y <u>cuánto</u> me han ayudado tus apuntes

25–26 ¡<u>Cuánto</u> tiempo sin vernos! ¿Qué me cuentas?

27–28 No sé cuándo [correct] ni dónde la volveré a ver

29–30 ¿Sabía su marido, que [no accent] tanto la quería, por <u>qué</u> lo había abandonado?

Day 5
POLITICS AND CURRENT AFFAIRS

1 ¿A qué hora . . . ?

2 el Consejo de Ministros . . .

3 . . . el presupuesto

4 sé que . . .

5 los organismos no gubernamentales . . .

6 . . . votar

7 Primer Ministro . . .

8 . . . gobierno minoritario . . .

9 . . . electorado

10 la Cámara de los Lores

11 ¿ . . . quién . . . ?

12 A . . . votar . . .

13 . . . las elecciones generales

14 un mitin . . .

15 . . . eligió . . .

16 . . . un nuevo líder

17 un/una tecnócrata

18 un/una burócrata

19 un/una dictador/-ora

20 dictatorial

21 el anarquismo

22 un/una anarquista

23 Deep down [or 'at heart'] . . .

24 . . . he/she is a right-wing politician

25 . . . notwithstanding his/her centre-left image

26 el conserva<u>d</u>urismo

27 British conservatism is quite unlike the political right in the United States

28 Schools in the state sector tend to have larger classes than those in the private sector

29 ecua<u>t</u>orial

30 In equatorial Africa, tribalism can be more important than political ideology

Day 6 REGULAR VERBS

1 cante (present subjunctive because of <u>querer</u> <u>que</u>)

2 viven

3 levanto

4 crees

5 pase lo que pase [present subjunctive because of 'what<u>ever</u>' meaning; 'forma reduplicativa']

6 hab<u>l</u>é, com<u>í</u>, viv<u>í</u>

7 hablaste, comiste, viviste
8 habló, comió, vivió
9 hablamos, comimos, vivimos
10 hablasteis, comisteis, vivisteis
11 hablaron, comieron, vivieron
12 hablara, comiera, viviera
13 hablaras, comieras, vivieras
14 hablara, comiera, viviera
15 habláramos, comiéramos, viviéramos
16 hablarais, comierais, vivierais
17 hablaran, comieran, vivieran
18 baile
19 bebías
20 sorprendió
21 mirará
22 peleamos
23 subierais
24 han discutido
25 besaban
26 Juan llegó . . .
27 . . . ¿Sabe usted qué hora es? . . .
28 . . . respondió Juan . . .
29 . . . que un chico le hablara . . .
30 . . . se disculpa . . .

Day 7 THE VISUAL ARTS
1 fotogénico
2 el fotomontaje [did you get the 'j' in the ending from words like garaje?]
3 la fotosíntesis
4 fit in with/are in keeping with/are in line with/are part of
5 was engraved/indelibly stamped on his memory
6 cuadrafónico
7 el/la acuarelista
8 escultar
9 smiling faintly/giving a hint of a smile
10 brush-strokes

11 cincelar
12 el/la retratista
13 a close-up
14 la negrura
15 greyish
16 greenish
17 to turn or look green

```
B E A C U A R E L A R G
L N P I G R A B A D O Y
A M I F G C J E H D J R
N A N E G R U Z C O I P
Q R A L M A L V A S Z A
U C C I R T B S A F O R
E A O E S B O Z A R L D
A R T N F Y I G U E T O
R Z E Z C A Q U I T U I
E C C O R E T R A T O T
L A A Y J F D E S H J I
```

18 la acuarela – water-colour
19 blanquear – to whiten or bleach
20 caqui – khaki
21 enmarcar – to frame
22 esbozar – to sketch
23 el grabado – engraving
24 el lienzo – canvas
25 malva – mauve
26 negruzco – blackish
27 pardo – brownish grey
28 la pinacoteca – art gallery
29 el retrato – portrait
30 rojizo – reddish

Day 8
ACCENTS: PART 1 – STRESS
1 ridículo
2 dijo
3 correct
4 hablaron
5 enorme
6 correct
7 análisis
8 correct
9 Dolores
10 correct
11 correct

12 correct
13 oído
14 buitre
15 cruel
16 veintidós
17 búhos
18 panaderías
19 lápices
20 ratones
21 ingleses
22 pianos
23 lámparas
24 leones
25 políticos
26 ministerios
27 grabaciones
28 aristócratas
29 fotografías
30 mítines

Day 9 LITERATURE
1 el monólogo
2 el diálogo
3 el narrador
4 el desenlace
5 la moraleja
6 agonizante
7 volver la página
8 el argumento
9 el personaje
10 rimar con
11 la aliteración
12 la asonancia
13 onomatopoeia
14 onomatopoeic
15 rítmico
16 la composición
17 octosyllable
18 hendecasyllable
19 el simbolismo
20 simbolista
21 simbólico
22 surrealista
23–30 Crossword answers (half a point for each completely correct one; no points if gender, spelling or accents are wrong!); for related terms, refer back to the lists in the section

Across:
1. la comedia musical
3. hacer mutis
6. el papeleo
8. entre bastidores
11. la sílaba
12. el dramaturgo
15. la comedia
Down
1. locuaz
2. el escenario
4. representar
5. la
7. teatral
9. estrenar
10. el poema
13. mudo
14. el

Day 10 SER AND ESTAR
1 es (noun complement)
2 es (noun complement)
3 estaba (continuous tense)
4–5 son (noun complement), son (inherent quality)
6 tengo ganas de
7 ando . . . corto/–a de
8 enfureció / enfurecía (both possible)
9 da pánico
10 se quedaron horrorizados/–as
11 quedando estrechos
12 guapa estás
13 es español
14 éramos jóvenes
15 estoy contento/–a
16 tonto/–a eres
17 estés listo/–a (subjunctive because cuando is referring to future relative to time of speaking)
18 ¿Estás solo/–a?
19 Somos felices
20–21 eran guapas; era . . . guapa
22 es . . . egoísta
23 estaba muerto
24–25 era viejo; estaba cansado

26 estás loco
27 es . . . aburrido
28 estaban vivos
29 estaba enfadado
30 estaba . . . enferma

Day 11 GEOGRAPHY
1–2 las estribaciones, Sierra
3 riadas
4 la meseta
5–6 Sudamérica (Suramérica is possible too), norteños
7 El sudeste (sureste is possible too)
8 occidental
9 El mapamundi
10 meridionales
11–12 sueca, marroquí
13–14 veneciano/–a, florentino/–a
15 galesa
16 parisina
17–18 belgas, flamenco
19 neoyorquinos
20 Varsovia
21–30 Check against the vocabulary list that precedes the exercise (page 60–61).

Day 12 – TIME
1 I had been living . . .
2 For how long have you been learning . . . ?
3 He has been dead (for) . . .
4 Hace muchos años que no toco el piano
No toco el piano desde hace muchos años
Llevo mucho años sin tocar el piano
5 Hacía varias semanas que nadie lo viera
Nadie lo veía desde hacía varias semanas
6 Hace un siglo que no hago esto
No hago esto desde hace un siglo
Llevo un siglo sin hacer esto

7 Hacía veinte años al menos que no iba al circo
No iba al circo desde hacía veinte años al menos
Llevaba veinte años al menos sin ir al circo
8 Hace seis años que estudio español
Estudio español desde hace seis años
Llevo seis años estudiando español
9 ¿Cuánto tiempo vas a pasar en España?
10 Durante quince años vivió en Venecia
11 . . . durante mucho tiempo
12 . . . donde pasaré un mes
13 . . . durante la noche
14 Siéntate un momento/segundo . . .
15 Momentito; ahora le paso el Sr. González
16 Por un momento/segundo me pareció ridículo todo . . .
17 para: possible
antes de: preferable
a: wrong (because it means 'at 7 o'clock')
18 para: possible
en: wrong in all circumstances ('on Friday' would simply be el viernes)
antes del viernes: preferable
19 Para: correct
Antes de: wrong (sounds most peculiar in Spanish!)
De: wrong (makes no sense)
20 Estas piedras seculares
21 el jueves que viene no, el otro
22 En menos de tres semanas
23 Quince días, una quincena
24 Los años cincuenta

25 De aquí un mes
26 Ocho días, una semana
27 Dentro de un año
28 De hoy en ocho días
29 Un malestar finisecular
30 . . . hace cinco siglos

Day 13 RHETORICAL SIGNPOSTS

1–2 no obstante . . . De ahí que
3–4 Sin embargo . . . Cabe pensar
5 en términos generales
6 por lo tanto
7 para colmo
8–9 Por otra parte . . . Menos mal
10–11 Por consiguiente . . . Evidentemente
12 en efecto
13–14 Por un lado . . . por otro . . . En cambio
15–16 Además . . . a diferencia de
17–18 dicho sea de paso . . . Como cabía esperar
19–22 En resumen . . . tanto . . . como . . . asimismo . . . por suerte
23–30 Match to list in section

Day 14 HISTORY

1, 2 el + either primero or a number from 2 to 31 (see list A below for spellings) + de + month (list B) + de + year (list C)

List A – NB if you have missed an accent, no marks!

dos	nueve
tres	diez
cuatro	once
cinco	doce
seis	trece
siete	catorce
ocho	quince

dieciséis	veinticuatro
diecisiete	veinticinco
dieciocho	veintiséis
diecinueve	veintisiete
veinte	veintiocho
veintiuno	veintinueve
veintidós	treinta
veintitrés	treinta y uno

List B – NB no initial capitals for months in Spanish
enero
febrero
marzo
abril
mayo
junio
julio
agosto
septiembre (or setiembre)
octubre
noviembre
diciembre

List C
mil novecientos + decade and year (for numbers up to 31 see list A above. From 31 onwards, the decade and the year are written as separate words connected by y as you saw in treinta y uno).
cuarenta
cincuenta
sesenta
setenta
ochenta
noventa
+ y + uno, dos, tres, etc.

A few examples:
el veinticinco de mayo de mil novecientos setenta y seis
el primero de octubre de mil novecientos noventa y uno
el dieciséis de enero de mil novecientos cincuenta y nueve

3, 10 When the day of the week is given, note that you lose the el before the date. No initial capitals for days of the week in Spanish:
lunes
martes
miércoles (no accent, no mark!)
jueves
viernes
sábado (same here)
domingo

Examples:
miércoles, cinco de abril de dos mil dos
sábado, primero de mayo de dos mil tres
lunes, veintiocho de diciembre de dos mil uno

4 Quinientos veintitrés antes de Jesucristo
5 Mil cuatrocientos noventa y dos
6 Mil ochocientos noventa y ocho
7, 8 For kings, queens, and popes, NB no definite article in Spanish preceding the number. Use ordinal numbers up to and including the tenth, then cardinals, as in the examples:
El Rey Enrique VIII (read Enrique Octavo)
El Rey Alfonso XII (read Alfonso Doce)
9 Mil novecientos veintisiete
10 See 3 above
11 el guerrero – warrior
la guerrilla (fem.) – guerrilla warfare
el/la guerrillero/-a – guerrilla fighter
12 imperial – imperial
imperar – to rule, prevail
imperante – prevailing (adj.)

imperioso – imperious
el emperador – emperor
la emperatriz – empress

13 la edad de oro – the
Golden Age
la edad de bronce – the
Bronze Age
la edad de piedra – the
Stone Age
la edad media – the
Middle Ages

14 victorioso – victorious
invicto – undefeated,
unbeaten

15 invencible – invincible,
unbeatable
el/la vencedor/-ora – the
winner, victor

16 el virrey – viceroy
la reina – queen
el reino – kingdom
reinar – to reign

17 subyugar – to subjugate

18 fronterizo – adj. for border
(controles o disputas
fronterizos/-as)

19 cortés – courteous, polite
el/la cortesano/-a –
courtier
la cortesana – courtesan
Las Cortes – Spanish
Parliament

20 la riqueza – wealth
la pobreza – poverty
la nobleza – nobility

21 la antigüedad –
antiquity, antique, seniority

22 el sirviente, la sirvienta –
servant
servicial – helpful
servil – servile

23 la esclavitud – slavery,
bondage

24 la heroína – heroine,
heroin
el heroísmo – heroism
heroico – heroic

25 el/la revolucionario/-a –
revolutionary
contrarrevolucionario –

counterrevolutionary

26 luchar con – to struggle
la lucha de las clases –
class struggle

27 rebelarse contra – to
rebel against
el/la rebelde – rebel

28 sin tregua – relentless(ly)

29 apaciguar – to pacify,
soothe
apacible – peaceable, calm
pacífico – pacific

30 histórico – historic,
historical (no accent, no
mark!)
el/la historiador/-ora –
historian

Day 15
RADICAL-CHANGING VERBS

1 la rueda – wheel
Radical-changing? – Yes

2 el remo – oar
Radical-changing?– No

3 el cuento – short story
Radical-changing? – Yes

4 medí

5 te diviertes

6 entendiera

7 soltará

8 refiriéramos

9 pidáis

10 solían

11 sierre

12 erras

13 herrará (but it is radical-
changing, as you might
have guessed from el
hierro)

14 cerraba (also radical-
changing; cf. el cierre –
close, as in close of trading
on the stock market)

15 hiriera

16 cubrimos

17 sintáis

18 riñen

19 vistiendo

20 pudrieron
colgar – to hang (up)

conferir (2) – to confer
(pattern 'guessable' from
referir)
defender – to defend
doler – to hurt
embestir (3) – to charge at
impedir (3) – to prevent
invertir (2) – to invest
moverse – to move, wag
presentir (2) – to have a
presentiment
resolver – to resolve

21 confiriendo

22 movió (if referring to a
particular occasion), or
movía (if it is what the dog
always used to do)

23 invirtió

24 colgó

25 duele

26 resolverían

27 embistió

28 presintió

29 defiendes

30 impidiéramos

Day 16 MUSIC

1 Concertar and desconcertar
are radical-changing

2 la armónica (no accent, no
mark!)

3 armonioso

4 la armonización

5 un/una afinador/-ora de
pianos

```
L A U R M V Y N N D E N
D I E L/A C O R D E J U
L O L G I A L E R S D E
E N C L I N J G L C E L
O E O E Z T R R H O S A
C D M E B A X A B N A R
E O P V A R O B C C F E
P Y Á S P Í J A L E I A
Q U S D A N C R U R N D
O R Q U E S T A L T A I
O N B U A T I P L A D O
R T O B J H N S D N O M
L A/A R M O N Í A T R I
A D I R I G I R E E O R I
```

6–15 Refer to lists preceding exercise
16 el/la guitarrista
17 el/la violinista
18 el/la trompetista
19 el/la clarinetista
20 el/la flautista
21 el disco compacto
22 . . . les gusta tanto a los intelectuales como a los iletrados
23 . . . los discos compactos 'Grandes Éxitos' (Remember capital letters in Spanish still have their accents.)
24 Ya no toco muy bien la guitarra . . .
25 . . . la letra de muchas canciones . . .
26 El nuevo batería del grupo . . .
27 . . . la 'España de pandereta' . . .
28 . . . el rey del rocanrol
29 A mi hijo de tres años se le regaló un tambor, . . .
30 . . . el chelo es uno de los instrumentos más románticos

Day 17
DEPENDENT PREPOSITIONS
1 . . . se me olvidó . . .
2 . . . ni siquiera me pagó una taza de café
3 Me acerqué a la mesa . . . (No mark if you forgot to change the c to qu!)
4 . . . consiste en dos apartamentos separados
5 Si de mí dependiera . . . (Notice that word order and try to remember to use it yourself.)
6 No me acuerdo de mi abuela . . .
7 Llamo a mis padres . . .
8 . . . nunca miras los letreros
9 . . . jugar al fútbol
10 Si te pide dinero . . .
11 Puedes confiar en mí . . .
12 Esperaba el tranvía desde hacía veinticinco minutos
13 Se arrepintió de su crueldad . . . (No mark if you missed the radical change!)
14 Me quejé del retraso . . .
15 Buscó la cara de su hijo . . .
16 Estaba hablando con el director de orquesta . . .
17 Me enteré de ello . . .
18 . . . todo el mundo me dice que me parezco más a mi madre (No mark if the irregular verb-form is wrong)
19–20 No te fíes de la memoria; apúntalo, que si no, se te olvidará
21 a) Vio la guitarra
22 a) La vio – (direct object)
23 b) Se parece a una estatua griega
24 b) Se le parece
25 a) El protagonista mata una mosca
26 a) El protagonista la mata en el último capítulo
27 b) Ramón llama al banco todos los días
28 b) Ramón le llama todos los días
29 a) Ramón besa la Biblia todas las noches
30 a) Ramón la besa todas las noches

Day 18 CINEMA
1 la cinematografía ('guessable' from other words with same ending, such as fotografía)
2 cinematográfico (cf. fotográfico)
3 cinemático (cf. automático)
4 subtitular
5 una película del Oeste
6 una película de vaqueros
7 la película de miedo (no accent, no mark!)
8 la pantalla grande

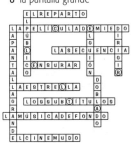

9 la música de fondo
10 los subtítulos
11 la secuencia
12 el cine mudo
13 la estrella
14 el público
15 el reparto
16 censurar
17 dirigir
18 doblado
19 el guión
20 el cartel – poster
21–22 Si no te acuerdas de su número de teléfono, consulta la guía

23–24 Arturo estaba repartiendo los naipes; jugábamos al póquer . . .

25–26 . . . dejé caer un huevo que se estrelló contra las baldosas
–Se lo pagaré de mi propio dinero . . .

27–28 . . . dobló las servilletas, quejándose de la falta de propina

29 . . . Quiero echar un vistazo a los titulares

30 . . . una lámpara con pantalla malva . . .

Day 19 IRREGULAR VERB
1 dijo
2 correct
3 correct
4–5 escribió . . . salió
6 puso
7 descrito
8 devuelto
revuelto
envuelto
desenvuelto
9 self-reliant, adult (in sense of mature), well-balanced (think of someone wrapped in the cocoon of childhood who has successfully emerged from and developed beyond that stage)
10 (yo) tradujera
(tú) tradujeras
(él) tradujera
(nosotros) tradujéramos
(vosotros) tradujerais
(ellos) tradujeran
11 (yo) reduje
(tú) redujiste
(él) redujo
(nosotros) redujimos
(vosotros) redujisteis
(ellos) redujeron
12 (yo) deduzca
(tú) deduzcas
(él) deduzca

(nosotros) deduzcamos
(vosotros) deduzcáis
(ellos) deduzcan
13 (yo)
dijera   trajera
(tú)
dijeras   trajeras
(él)
dijera   trajera
(nosotros)
dijéramos   trajéramos
(vosotros)
dijerais   trajerais
(ellos)
dijeran   trajeran
14 First-person singular of present indicative and all the way through present subjunctive
15 Pres. ind.   Pres. subj.
(yo)
caigo   caiga
(tú)
caes   caigas
(él)
cae   caiga
(nosotros)
caemos   caigamos
(vosotros)
caéis   caigáis
(ellos)
caen   caigan
16 Gerund/present participle, third-person singular and plural of preterite and therefore, all the way through the imperfect subjunctive
17 (yo) dije
18 (tú) pudiste
19 (él) oyó
20 (ella) retraiga
21 (Vd.) maldice
22 (nosotros) deduzcamos
23 (vosotros) releyerais
24 (ellos) cayeran
25 (ellas) anduvieron
26 (Vds) creyendo
27 Nos dio entradas . . .
28 Fui a ver una nueva

película . . .
29–30 Vio a Antonio Banderas . . . cuando fue al estreno . . .

Day 20 EDUCATION
1 la escuela primaria
2 la profesión (cf. la discusión)
3 clasificar (no double 's' in Spanish, remember)
4 las facultades mentales
5 el universo
6 universal
7 estudioso
8–9 ¿Cuántos alumnos internos hay en este colegio?
10–12 La vida estudiantil consiste en más que estudiar
13–14 Se ha instituido un nuevo sistema según el cual los profesores no sabrán de quiénes son los exámenes que están corrigiendo
15 . . . ha perdido sus facultades mentales casi por completo
16–17 De jóvenes, yo y un par de compañeros de clase hacíamos novillos . . .
18–19 No suele haber uniforme en los institutos pero sí en los colegios de monjas
20 Invitan a los antiguos alumnos . . .
21 Después de la universidad . . .
22 Estaba ausente cuando nos explicó la lección 14, pero la estudié en casa después
23 ¡Enhorabuena! You passed all your exams? Congratulations!
24 incorregible
How many times have I

told you not to dirty the tablecloth with your paints? And you don't take the slightest notice! You are incorrigible!

25 repaso
Do you know this book? It's helping me a good deal; it consists of a general revision programme focusing on the hardest points

26 suspenden
At my school if you fail more than three subjects you have to repeat the year

27 decurso
They loved each other a lot when they got married, but over the years their love gradually faded

28 desapruebas
I can see by your face that you disapprove of my idea

29 corregir
Some teachers take weeks to correct their pupils' homework

30 noto
You look very tired; you've been up all night working again, haven't you?

Day 21
CONDITIONAL SENTENCES

1 i
2 iii
3 v
4 iv
5 ii
6-7 Si me lo hubieras dicho antes, habría podido ayudarte
7–8 Si llegamos tarde, mis padres se enfadarán
8–9 Si tú estuvieras aquí ahora, ¡cuánto nos divertiríamos juntos!
10–11 Si tú hubieras estado escuchando cuando te lo

explicó, no nos habríamos perdido
12–13 Si yo fuera tu padre, no estarías diciéndome cosas así
14–15 Si estás hablando por teléfono cuando llegue yo, te esperaré en el coche
16 compulsory subj.
17 compulsory subj.
18 optional alternative to conditional
19 Lo habrías odiado, de haber estado
20 De haberme acordado a tiempo, habría dicho algo
21–22 Si no me gustaras, te lo diría
23–24 Teníamos que ir a misa todos los domingos, y si llegábamos tarde, las monjas nos castigaban
25–26 Si le explicas por qué llegaste tarde, no te reñirá
27–28 De haberlo sabido, no se habría enfadado
29–30 Era ridículo, si era comprensible, que les tuviéramos tanto miedo

Day 22 HEALTH

1 flu-like symptoms
2 alérgico
3 la salud pública (no mark if you forgot the agreement!)
4 el/la canceroso/-a
5 cosmetic surgery
6 el/la anestesista
7 anestesiar
8a la cirugí
8b la varicel
9a la alergi
9b la vacun
10a la anestesi
10b el sid
11a la enfermer
11b anestesist
12a la jaquec
12b práctic
13a enfermiz

13b el disos
14a el quirófan
14b elérgic
15a canceros
15b el sarpullid
16a el resfriad
16b el infart
17a la grip
17b el síndrom
18a practicant
18b saludabl
19a la fiebr
19b el sarampión
20 pneumonia
21 la bronquitis
22 la artritis
23 una otitis
24 la amigdalitis
25 Llevaron a los heridos al hospital
26 ¿Cómo funciona la seguridad social en Inglaterra?
27–28 El médico me recetó unas gotas para la [or mi] otitis
29 A los niños de hoy ya no se suele sacarles las amígdalas
30 Estuve un mes en la cama a causa de una pulmonía

Day 23 DIALOGUE

1 saludó
2 respondí
3 preguntó
4 mascullé
5 prosiguió
6 interrumpí
7 refunfuñó
8 chilló
9 susurró
10 balbuceé
11 bramó
12 replicó
13 exclamé
14 gimió (or gemía, if context was that she was moaning it over and over again for an extended period)

15 opuso
16 incrédulo – incredulously
17 con resentimiento – resentfully
18 con voz trémula – shakily
19 riendo – 'laughingly' not really suitable here since so often used sarcastically these days (as in 'what is laughingly known as . . . '). Best option would probably be to say 'she laughed' instead of 'she replied' + adverb
20 –¡Hola! ¿Qué haces tú por aquí? Yo te creía en Inglaterra – dijo Inma sorprendida . . .
21 –¡Hola! Estuve en Inglaterra, en efecto, pero estoy de vuelta desde hace una semana ya – le respondí
22–23 –¿Por ejemplo? – preguntó / interpuso Inma. Dijo with the accent crossed off, is acceptable mark for the inversion, one for the verb
24–25 –¿Y los londinenses? interrogó Inma sonriendo / con una sonrisa (or simply) sonrió Inma
26–27 dijo / comentó con sarcasmo
28 –¡Qué va! – le dije / respondí yo
29 –Sí, gracias. Oye – se interrumpió . . .
30 añadí / agregué

Day 24
SPELLING CHANGES
1 venzo – I defeat (First person singular of present indicative)
venza, venzas, venza, venzamos, venzáis, venzan (whole of present subjunctive)

2 busqué
3 pescas
4 consiga
5 rugiendo
6 escojáis
7 convencían
8 averigüé, apacigüé
9 el agua
10 el güisqui
11 la tregua
12 la vergüenza
13 el guardia
14 el gueto
15 la guerrilla
16 el gorila
17 el guijarro
18 el cero
19 la cebra
20 el parque zoológico
21 zurdo
22 el cigarrillo
23 el lazo
24 el desenlace
25 el queso
26 la cuestión
27 ¿cuánto?
28 la cualidad
29 Quito
30 equivalente

Day 25 SCIENCE
1 The tree of knowledge of good and evil
2 metafísico
3 la física nuclear
4 un/una químico/-a
5 genetic engineering
6 teológico, la teología, el/la teólogo/-a
7 astrológico, la astrología, el/la astrólogo/ -a
8 antropológico, la antropología, el/la antropólogo/-a
9 test-tube baby
10 contaminar
11 el efecto invernadero
12 el gas invernadero
13 progresar
14–16 En la escuela, prefería

la física a la química, pero en cuanto a la biología, no la aguantaba
17 . . . es tan concienzudo . . .
18–19 . . . lo que nos dicen los científicos sobre el efecto invernadero
20 No creo en la astrología.
21 . . han hecho grandes progresos . . .
22–23 Los proyectos de investigación científica . . .
24–25 Los antropólogos no se limitan a investigar sobre los pueblos primitivos
26–27 . . . es peligroso consumir productos químicos en la comida; hay que probarlo
28 La contaminación del Mar Mediterráneo . . .
29–30 Los avances en genética dan miedo a algunos, que hablan de experimentación al estilo de Frankenstein

Day 26 IMPERATIVES
1 ¡No hables!
2 ¡No comáis!
3. ¡Beba esto!
4 ¡No beba eso!
5 ¡Corran !
6 ¡No corran!
7 Dime cómo acaba la película
8 Hazme caso
9 Ponte ese sombrero
10 Ven a verme esta tarde
11 Sé bueno
12 Baila conmigo
13 No me llames después de las once
14 Lea el texto en voz alta
15 Ruégueles que se sienten ahora
16 Convénzanme
17 Salid al jardín si queréis jugar al fútbol
18 Búscalo

19 Correct
20 Cómpramelo
21 tú: no me des un beso
22 vosotros: no vengáis a cenar mañana
23 ustedes: no se levanten por favor
24 vosotros: no os acostéis en seguida
25 usted: no haga seguir mi correo a mi nueva dirección
26 vosotros: ¡No os vayáis ahora mismo!
27 Vamos a comer ahora
28 No comamos antes de que lleguen
29 Vamos a esperarles
30 No les esperemos

Day 27
SIMILES AND SET EXPRESSIONS
All answers can be easily checked from the vocabulary lists provided within this section (see pages 149–51).

Day 28
SOME MINOR POINTS
1 padre e hijo
2 Correct
3 Quince o veinte (because written in words, not figures)
4 Virgilio u Homero
5 25 ó 26
6 Correct (because hierba is pronounced 'yerba', cf. hielo)
7 francófonos e hispanoparlantes.
8 La película tiene lugar en la América (fem.) de los años veinte (initial 'a' is not stressed)
9 El delfín es un animal muy inteligente (animal is masc., but anyway the initial 'a' is not stressed)

10 Tu discurso me ha llegado hasta el alma (fem.) (stressed /a/)
11 El haba (fem.) es un legumbre delicioso (stressed /a/)
12 La vida de un ama de casa (fem.) puede ser frustrante (stressed /a/)
13 Murió cuando se cortó una arteria (fem.) principal en un accidente industrial (initial 'a' is not stressed)
14 Tenemos que combatir el hambre (fem.) en el tercer mundo (stressed /a/)
15 El África del Sur (fem.) de hoy no tiene nada que ver con lo que era hace veinte años (stressed /a/)
16 Muchas gracias, eres un ángel – (ángel is always masc., even if applied metaphorically to a woman)
17 raramente
18 tontamente
19 maquinalmente
20 antiguamente
21 fácilmente
22 increíblemente
23 era tonta y locamente feliz
24 Estaba ciega, violenta, y salvajemente furioso
25 Dame media horita y estoy de vuelta
Just give me half an hour and I'll be straight back
26 Viven en una casucha sin jardín, en un barrio bajo de la ciudad
They live in a poky little house with no garden in a down-at-heel part of town
27 Al ver su carita sonriéndome, me sentí mejor en seguida
Just the sight of her little smiling face made me feel better at once

28 Hemos comprado una casita en la costa
We've bought a little house on the coast
29 Dale un besito a tu muñeca antes de acostarla
Give your doll a nice kiss before you put her to bed
30 La muy tonta soltó una risita porque no quería parecer pudibunda
The silly woman giggled because she didn't want to seem a prude

Day 29
VOCABULARY SELF-TEST
1 el pelo liso
2 encararse con
3 tacaño
4 gubernamental
5 el/la demócrata
6 de fácil trato
7 la pinacoteca
8 esbozar
9 carmesí
10 la sílaba
11 entre bastidores
12 las estribaciones
13 argelino
14 sin ambages
15 el imperio
16 sin tregua
17 desacorde
18 la pandereta
19 el guión
20 los titulares
21 el ausentismo
22 el curso
23 cancerígeno
24 la seguridad social
25 chillar
26 refunfuñar
27 el/la biólogo/-a
28 el invernadero
29 perder los estribos
30 como boca de lobo

Day 30
BASIC ERRORS SELF-TEST

1 1 error: demasiado [adverbial use of demasiado so no agreement – see Day 1]

2 2 errors: ¿quién? [accent needed for interrogative – see Day 4]; si hubieras podido [subjunctive needed in the 'if' clause – see Day 21]

3 3 errors: ¿ missing; quedan [normal pres. indicative needed of reg. verb – see Day 6]; una [gender of foto is feminine]

4 1 error: París [stress rules – see Day 8]

5 1 error: era [obligatory use of ser with noun complement – see Day 10]

6 3 errors: jamón twice [stress rules – see Day 8]; español [no capitals for adjectives of nationality – see Day 11]

7 3 errors: castellana [agreement – see Day 1]; desde hacía [must be in past because following past tense atravesaba – see Day 12]; vio [no accent here since 1959 – see Day 24]

8 Correct!

9 2 errors: desde hacía [stress rules – see Day 8]; veintidós [stress rules – see Day 8]

10 3 errors: mí [accent to distinguish pronoun from adjective – see Day 4]; absurda [agreement – see Day 1]; términos [stress rules – see Day 8]

11 2 errors: e historia [because of /i/ sound at beginning of next word – see Day 28]; más [accent to distinguish 'more' from 'but' – see Day 4]

12 2 errors: relación [stress rules – see Day 8]; delincuencia [spelling rules – see Day 24]

13 2 errors: sintió [radical-changing verb form – see Day 15]; una mano [unpredictable gender – see Day 27]

14 1 error: escocés [stress rules – see Day 8]

15 2 errors: dependerá [regular verb form – see Day 6]; de [unpredictable dependent preposition for depender – see Day 17]

16 1 error: habérmelo [stress rules – see Day 8]

17 1 error: Anduvo [irregular verb-forms – see Day 19]

18 Correct!

19 2 errors: Dijo [irregular verb-forms – see Day 19]; sí [accent to distinguish 'yes' from 'if' – see Day 4]

20 2 errors: consistía en [unpredictable dependant preposition for consistir – see Day 17]; África [stress rules and capital letters must have accents too in Spanish – see Day 8]

21 Correct!

22 1 error: Aquí [stress rules – see Day 8]

23 1 error: convénzaselo [mistake was to use tú-form imperative when rest of sentence uses usted – see Day 26 for imperatives and Day 24 for spelling change c/z]

24 2 errors: 80 ó 90 [accent needed between numbers written in figures – see Day 28]; prefirieron [radical-changing – see Day 15]

25 2 errors: genética [agreement – see Day 1] e importantes [y becomes e before word starting with /i/ sound – see Day 28]

26 1 error: Pídeselo [usted form of imperative used when 'tu padre' showed tú form was needed – see Day 26 for imperatives and Day 15 for radical-changing verbs]

27 1 error: digas [imperative needed – see Day 26]

28 2 errors: supe [irregular verb – see Day 19]; creérmelo [stress rules – see Day 8]

29 1 error: expliqué [spelling rules – see Day 24]

30 Correct!

Index

This index uses roman type to refer to explanatory coverage and practice of each point in *Upgrade*. Italics are used for references to pages where a point arises incidentally, in an exercise or vocabulary list. This index does not refer you to the answer section except where an explanation appears there.

accents 17–20, *161–3*; on adverbs 40, 155; in direct and indirect questions 17–20, *22–3*, 166; as distinguishing marks 17, *22*; in exclamations 17–18; on **o** ('or') 153–4; for stress 1, 17, 25, *32–3*, 37–41, *45, 78*, 101–2, 104, 108, 145

adjectives, agreement of 1–5, *8–9, 12, 14–15, 18–20, 55–6*, 154, 156, 161–3; invariable 2

adverbs 4, avoidance of 129, 156; formation of 40, 155–6

aticles, omission of 123, 169; use of masculine with feminine nouns 33, 59, 154, 175

capitalization 59, *161–3*, 169

checking 2, 4, *15, 20*, 29, 101–2, *130–31, 153–4*, 161–3

cognates 7, *11*, 31, *33–5*, 43, *44–6, 47–9, 61–2, 76–8*, 79, *85–8, 97, 111–13, 123–4, 137, 139*

conditional sentences 117–22, *161*

dates 68, 75–6, 168–9

demasiado 4, *161*, 165

dieresis, use of 135

diminutives and augmentatives 157

false friends *46, 69, 85, 114, 126*

gerund *see* present participle

guessing 7, 31–5, 43, *43–6*, 57, 79–80, *85, 97–8, 107, 111–13, 123–4, 137–9*

imperatives *12*, 143–7

inversion, after direct speech 130–31

morphology, as aid to guessing and learning vocabulary 7, 23–4, 31–4, 44–6, *88–9, 111, 124, 126, 137–8*

nouns, as complement 51, 53, *119, 162, 168*; ending in **–ma** 44, *47–9*, 154–5; gender of 33, *36, 45, 47–9*, 57–9, *61–2*, 154–5

numbers 75–6, 169, 175

o, ó, and u 153–4, *161–3*

orthographic changes *see* spelling rules

past participle, agreement of 3–4, 165; irregular forms of 102–3, 106, 109, *119*

prepositions 22, 60, 66–8, 91–6, 98, 111; **durante** 66; personal *a* 93–6; **pro/para** 66–7, 72

present participle/gerund *134*; irregular forms of 102, 106, *108*; no agreement of 3–4, 165; radical changes 80–81, *82*

pronouns, direct vs. indirect 91, 93–6, as suffixes 145

punctuation *161–3*

ser and **estar** 51–6, *119*, *162*, 168

spelling rules 133–6; **c, cu, qu,** and **z** 1, 31, *40*, 60, 77, 92, 98, 124, 127, 133–6, 139; **g, gu, gü,** and **j** 77–8, 92, 127, *130*, 133–6, 139; vowels separated by **h** 40

stress, in preterite forms *27*, 101–2, 104, 106–8; *see also* accents

subjunctive, formation of 27, *28*, 80–81, 102–8, 133–4; **–ra** form replacing conditional 120; recognition of 14, *15*; uses of 13–15, *16*, 69, 114, 117–22, 143, 166, 168

time and duration 63–8

verbs *161–3*, dependent prepositions with *23*, 91–6, *100*; irregular 27, 29, *93*, 101–9, *119*, *121–2*, *127–8*, 144; radical-changing *23*, 29, 44, 57, 79–83, *85*, *93*, 114, *119*, *122*, 126–8, 138, 144, 149; regular 25–9, *119*, *121–2*, *126–8*, *134–5*, *143*

vocabulary *see* contents for lexical domains; learning strategies 4, 7, 20, 21, 81, 90, 115, 141, 149, 152, 159–60; *see also* false freinds

y and **e** 153–154, *161–163*, 175